# Salsa Dancing In Gym Shoes

*Developing Cultural Competence to Foster Latino Student Success*

## 2nd Edition

Tammy Oberg De La Garza

Alyson L. Lavigne

# DEDICATION

We dedicate this book to past, present, and future teachers who create safe, engaging, and equitable places for students to learn, question, and thrive.

# CONTENTS

**Acknowledgments**        i

**Preface**        1

**Part ONE – Learning the Steps of a New Dance**

Chapter 1: Surveying the Dance Floor        Pg. 9

Chapter 2: Learning to Dance at Home        Pg. 15

Chapter 3: Identity and Personal Experiences        Pg. 40

Chapter 4: Treatment as Individuals        Pg. 62

**Part TWO - Dancing in Culture**

Chapter 5: Accessing Culture through Language        Pg. 93

Chapter 6: Language Deliberations and Power        Pg. 114

Chapter 7: Language Instruction Models        Pg. 138

Chapter 8: Taking the Dance Floor by Storm        Pg. 167

**References**        Pg. 171

# ACKNOWLEDGMENTS

We  would like to thank our families. Without their love and support, this book would not have been possible. Much gratitude is extended to our colleagues and students at Roosevelt University and Utah State University, who challenge us to be better leaders, teachers, and human beings.  Many thanks to Andrea Bastien for helpful editing contributions.

# PREFACE:
# LEARNING THE STEPS
# OF A NEW DANCE

*We may have different religions, different languages, different colored skin, but we all belong to one human race.*

~Kofi Annan~

Ghana Diplomat, 2001 Nobel Peace Prize Winner

Warning: if you wish to Salsa dance, NEVER wear gym shoes! Salsa dancing is a Latin dance style associated with Salsa music that has worldwide popularity, particularly in Latin America and the United States. The music is a rhythmic fusion of Cuban, African, and Caribbean influences. Salsa's addictive quality is appealing because it is relatively easy to learn and is not constrained by many parameters. The dancer is free to do almost anything as long as he or she masters the basic three-weight-change steps. During the dance, the upper body remains nearly unaffected by the weight transfers and involves a lot of hip movement.

Understandably, the shoes of a Salsa dancer must enable a wearer to brush the floor while providing enough grip to prevent slipping and falling. Salsa shoes are typically comfortable and flexible, with soles made of real suede or leather to provide the perfect balance of glide and traction on the dance floor. Too much grip would restrict the foot pivot and likely cause awkward movements, missteps, falls, and/or knee damage. For this reason, rubber-soled sneakers are not a good option for Salsa dancing.

We use the analogy of Salsa Dancing in Gym Shoes to represent the awkward, sometimes damaging interactions that take place where cultural patterns differ. Becoming familiar with new cultural patterns is similar to learning dance steps or dancing with a new partner. Like wearing the proper footwear to Salsa dance, classroom teachers, equipped with the right knowledge, can begin to understand and avoid missteps with their culturally diverse students. Cultural mismatches, like wearing gym shoes to Salsa dance, might cause even the best teacher to stumble and possibly fall on his or her face.

Misunderstood cultural variations incubate tension in relationships. I (Tammy Oberg De La Garza) am White, and early in my marriage to my Mexican American husband, he frequently asked me why my Anglo parents didn't like him. Regardless of the affection they felt, their respectful yet stoic handshake greeting was in sharp contrast to the warm *abrazo* (hug) and *beso* (kiss) I received from his mother each time she greeted me. This cultural difference became a source of contention and frequently surfaced during our newlywed disagreements. My husband felt rejected by the friendly yet formal interactions with my family—the very same interactions I interpreted as growing fondness and genuine affection. It became my responsibility to translate the perceived neutral and cool behaviors of my White culture into the parallel yet more expressive patterns of engagement found in his Latino culture.

All the while, I was learning that the inviting smile and gregarious hugs that consistently welcomed me into his circle of family and friends didn't automatically mean that I was deeply appreciated or accepted by the sender. In my family and circle of friends, hugs and kisses were reserved for deeply connected or intimate relationships. I also learned to accept that the concept

2

of time differed between our cultures and that a late arrival to my carefully planned Christmas dinner didn't necessarily equate with aversion or disrespect.

These cultural missteps initially made it challenging to feel completely accepted and safe in our relationship. This gap in behavioral operations threatened our capabilities of relating to each other, requiring a leap of faith or a bridge to connect the cultures before we could ease into a rhythm of married life. Like dancers learning the steps to a new dance, we became more familiar with the initially awkward patterns of cultural engagement. Over time we learned how to read and navigate the differences in our cultural traditions. As our confidence grew, we became more fluid and graceful in understanding new and diverse situations. Like skillful dancers anticipating movements capable of causing a partner to stumble, my beloved husband and I learned how to steer and guide each other through potentially difficult circumstances.

I've been on the dance floor of marriage for nearly as many years as I've been an educator. In the two decades I've spent as first a fourth-grade teacher, literacy coach, and provider of profession- al development, and now a teacher educator, I recognize a parallel in the cultural missteps that are being made in the classroom. Although no teacher would consciously construct an experience for students to cause conflict or discomfort, cultural differences create the context that is abundant with opportunity for misinterpretation—similar to that in my early years of marriage. The ways in which cultural differences are navigated between Whites and Latinos are clumsy at best, dangerous at worst, and much like wearing gym shoes while dancing the Salsa.

## USING THIS BOOK TO NAVIGATE TWO WORLDS

*Salsa Dancing in Gym Shoes* considers how cultural missteps between classroom teachers and their students play a role in hindering Latinos from meeting basic standards in urban classrooms. This book is a 360° journey through Latino culture, history, identity, and language in the home, the individual, and the classroom. This experiential tour will guide you through research, personal narratives, and classroom instruction in pivotal ways that impact heart, mind, and practice. Critical themes explore bias, human development, and classroom instruction, inviting you to successfully navigate the uncharted territory between yourself and the Latino students you teach.

When learning the beautiful and intricate steps of a new dance, it isn't uncommon to step on a partner's toes. *Salsa Dancing in Gym Shoes* uses the analogy of dance to portray the unspoken yet very real obstacles awaiting the 84 percent of public-school teachers whose Anglo culture is strikingly different—and at times clashes with the Latino experience. Before learning a new dance, one must be familiar with the appropriate footwear. The content of this book will give you an opportunity to stand in another's shoes awhile before moving to the dance floor.

Like novice dancers, one must accurately interpret and anticipate a partner's steps. Misunderstandings between Latinos and their White counterparts occur in homes, classrooms, and public spaces. This gap in cultural recognition causes missed opportunities for strong relationships, job advancement, and educational success. To better meet the educational needs of Latinos, we need to go beyond a vague acknowledgment of their culture. We must deliberately construct a new approach that enhances relationships, instead of diminishing them.

*Salsa Dancing in Gym Shoes* surveys the vacant dance floor between Latinos and Whites. Broken into three parts, each chapter explores different themes through the lens of (a) research and theory, (b) experience, and finally, (c) effective classroom practice. Drawn from teacher development research, the first part of each chapter gives readers the distinct opportunity to make connections between their educational experiences as a student and future or current educational situations as a teacher. To that end, this part provides the foundational knowledge needed to better understand the narrative that follows. The heart of every chapter features purposefully woven narratives by authors intimately familiar with issues of identity and culture that confront Latinos today. The essays vary widely in emotion, tone, perspective, experience, and writing styles. We have not edited the essayists' writing in order to preserve their individual style and voice. At times unpleasant, these essays raise critical questions that challenge readers to analyze their unexplored belief systems for potential bias. The third portion of each chapter, *Take It to the Classroom*, responds to the theme with practical tools that teachers can use to positively and effectively mold the classroom experience for all learners.

Guiding readers on a journey through cultural clashes, challenges, and breakthroughs, reflective prompts and "pop-outs" will ask you to reflect, understand, empathize, and analyze the implications of the essay. *Background Knowledge* pop-outs are placed in shaded text boxes to supplement schema with information about a concept or aspect of the essay with which you may be unfamiliar. For example, *Background Knowledge* may provide readers with details about historical events that were significant in shaping the lives of Latinos. These pop-outs can be read before, during, or after the essay. Another prompt, *Classroom Connections*, invites readers to visit and contemplate practical applications of ideas presented in the essay. These prompts can be reviewed during or after the reading of the essay. The third type of prompt is deliberately designed to disrupt the flow of reading and compel readers to pause and consider deeper implications of issues raised in the essay. *Critical Thinking* breaks are strategically presented to provide opportunities for new thinking, beliefs, and ideas to develop. These prompts may be used to ignite meaningful discussions in professional development settings or the teacher-preparation classroom.

## BOOK CONTENTS

This book is divided into two parts. In Part One-*Learning the Steps of a New Dance* (Chapters 2-4), we explore cultural missteps that have taken place in the lives of Latinos in the classroom and the workplace throughout history. Part Two-*Dancing in Culture* (Chapters 5-7), invites you to consider the role that language plays in culture, particularly as it will be the predominant aspect of culture over which teachers have influence in the classroom. In both parts of the book, the veiled, relational tension between Latinos and Whites takes center stage while a spotlight illuminates cultural differences.

In Chapter 2, you will explore the themes of home, family values, and cultural clashes. In her vivid essay, "A Latina Journey of Empowerment," Elena García Ansani, the daughter of Mexican immigrants, sets the stage of racial discrimination. The reader is given a front-row seat to the confusion and rejection of racism and prejudice. Viewed through the eyes of a child, this essay allows readers to empathize with the obstacles that shaped this strong, proud, and intelligent Latina. In the *Take It to the Classroom* portion of this chapter, the issue of battling racism through classroom practice is explored through the vehicle of classroom practice, instructional methodology, and resources for bias-free classrooms.

The theme in Chapter 3 turns to the individual and identity development, belonging, and student outcomes. The essay by Sarah Rafael García portrays a crushing classroom experience and the pain of assimilating to the White culture and becoming "culturally ambiguous." *Take It to the Classroom* presents the roles and opportunities for mainstream teachers to support student bicultural identity and belonging in the classroom, low-risk/high-impact instruction, and identity-friendly speaking and reading practices.

Chapter 4 delves into the difficult arena of culture and stereotypes. In the essay, Mayra Carrillo-Daniel introduces a wide span of cultural examples through language, cuisine, customs, holidays, values, dating, and music. Her narrative treats us to an outsider's perspective confronting elements of white culture that can be easily overlooked as definitively American. The *Take It to the Classroom* section tackles racism directly through the development of culturally responsive dispositions, teaching practices, and classrooms.

Chapter 5, *Accessing Culture Through Language* marks the beginning of Part Two and narrows our focus to language. Language serves as a gateway through the various aspects of culture, particularly it's pivotal role in culture. In his essay, Elvis Sánchez highlights the similarities between the Spanish and English languages, and uses the universality of rice as a bridge to connect cultures. In *Take It to the Classroom*, we follow Elvis's lead and turn to stories, libraries, and book practices to help others understand different cultures.

The theme of language deliberations at home is elaborated upon in Chapter 6. This chapter addresses parents' views and experiences with making decisions about language use at home, thus influencing the levels of bilingualism and biculturalism of their children. In her essay, Josie Prado shares her deliberate thought process and very personal decision about language usage at home with her biracial children. *Take It to the Classroom* illuminates the uneven platform that bilingual students face, and offers language and reading practices that foster a balanced bilingual identity. This singular identity approach combats the typical split-identity embraced by bilingual students who only speak Spanish at home and English at school.

Chapter 7 narrows the focus even more closely on bilingual

education and language-learning theory in the classroom. Bilingual and English as a Second Language (ESL) instruction that is specifically outlined in public policies doesn't always translate into classroom practice. The essay "Around Latin America in a Kite: an American Classroom" reflects this blurred delineation, when Laura Guzmàn-DuVernois paints the beautiful portrait of the lexical dance that takes place in her English-language-learning classroom. She demonstrates the skilled flexibility of a dancer, when teaching a seemingly straightforward lesson on the word "kite" explodes with the numerous varieties of words and their meanings within the Spanish language. In Take It to the Classroom, we explore critical elements of ESL instruction that should be part of every classroom—ESL, bilingual, and mainstream. Weaving this story with language as a craft, this author shares a hopeful example of what an ESL/bilingual classroom can be—a positive picture of acceptance and grace.

In this edition, we include updated data on student demographics in the United States. We incorporate evolving understandings about culturally sustaining practice (which has previously been referred to as culturally responsive pedagogy) and recent findings on the effectiveness of bilingual education, specifically dual language education.

We hope that this new edition challenges you to question your own assumptions, beliefs, and practices. We also hope this book allows you to identify and become more aware of cultural missteps inside and outside of the classroom while simultaneously developing a more nuanced understanding of the experiences and lives of the students you teach or will teach in the near future. The music is starting. Let the dance begin!

# CHAPTER 1
# SURVEYING THE DANCE FLOOR

*No silver bullet or single program can close the enormous gap between Latino students and their peers with respect to academic achievement and attainment. But it's in all of our interests to find ways to begin the process of narrowing those gaps.*

~Patricia Gándara~

Professor of education at UCLA, co-director of the civil rights project,
and co-author of *The Latino Education crisis*

## LATINOS IN THE UNITED STATES

The United States is made up of 56.6 million Latinos, two-thirds of which are of Mexican heritage (U.S. Census Bureau, 2016). The Latino population constitutes the largest minority group in the United States, representing 17.6 percent of the US population (U.S. Census Bureau 2016), and is growing. Between 2000 and 2016, the Hispanic population increased 62 percent – from 35.3 million to 56.6 million. To put this growth in perspective, there was only a 5 percent increase of the non-Hispanic population over the same period of time.

It comes as no surprise, that 25 percent of American children in grades K–12 are Latino, and in key southwestern states such as Texas and California, the Latino school-age population is already approaching one-half (NCES, 2017). Latino students are the largest, fastest-growing racially minoritized[1] group in US classrooms and projections show that by 2025, nearly 29 percent of public school students will be Latino (Humes, Jones, & Ramirez, 2011; NCES, 2017).

While the number of Latinos attending public schools has steadily increased over the past decades, the education levels of Latinos, however, are lower than any other minority group, and the dropout rates are the highest. Each year, nearly 50 percent of Latino high school students fail to graduate with their class, increasing their chances of not being able to find employment or receiving public assistance and living in poverty, in prison, and/or on death row (Buchanan, 2005).

In 2011, eighth-grade Latino students' scores on standardized reading measures were closer to fourth-grade white students than to their own eighth-grade peers (NCES, 2011). Figure 1.1 on the following page clearly demonstrates that though the reading scores of Hispanic and White students are increasing, the achievement gap has not significantly improved over a nineteen-year period.

---

[1] We use the term "racially minoritized" to recognize that race is socially constructed. In other words, people are not born "a minority status nor are they minoritized in every social context" (Harper, 2012, p. 9). Minority status emerges in contexts overrepresented by whiteness.

**4th Grade Reading Achievement**

**8th Grade Reading Achievement**

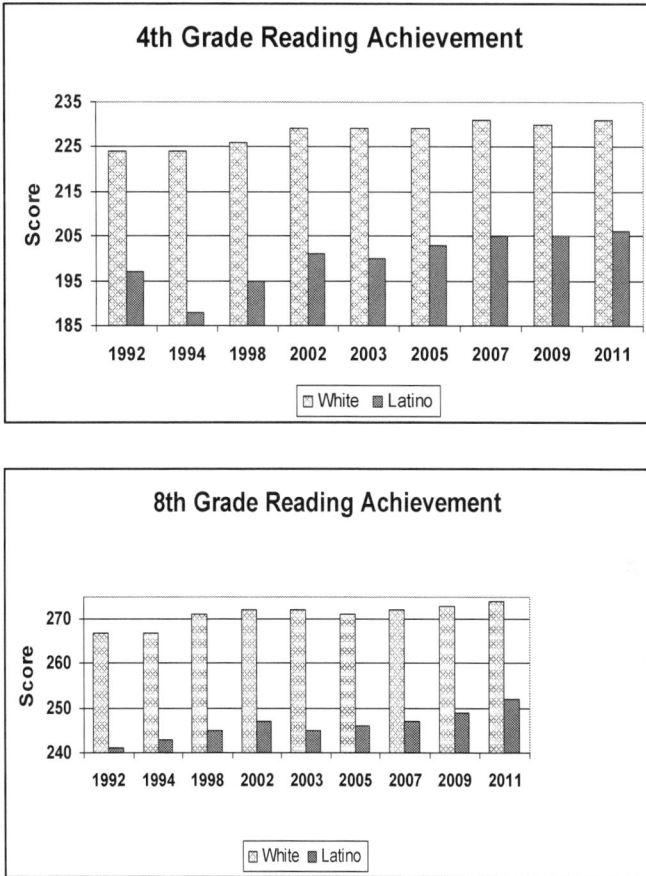

**Figure 1.1** *Achievement Gap – Latino/White*

The number of English Language Learners (ELLs) in public-school classrooms is also rising. In 1993-1994, there were 2.1 million ELLs, representing 5 percent of all public school students. By 2002-2004, the enrollment had steadily risen to 4.1 million or 9 percent of all students. By 2015-2016, the population of ELLs had expanded to 4.8 million students, accounting for nearly 10 percent of the student body (NEA, 2007; NCES, 2004, 2018). Roughly 77 percent of ELLs speak Spanish as their primary language (NCES, 2018).

On the surface, it would seem logical to rationalize that language and immigrant status would be the major detriment in academic success; however, studies comparing grades, test scores, and dropout rates show that immigrants outperform their US-born, English-speaking children, grandchildren, and great-grandchildren (Buriel, 1987; Buriel & Cardoza, 1988; Suárez-Orozco, 1991; Vigil & Long, 1981). In their longitudinal study, Hao and Woo (2012) followed 10,700 children ages 13–17 until the ages of 25–32 and found that foreign-born students who were brought to the United States outperformed second and third generations in educational, social, and behavioral outcomes. Despite challenges of dual cultural identity, limited language proficiency in English, poverty, and a racial minority status, there appears to be a "protective" mechanism of being foreign-born, particularly when it comes to performance in Science, Technology, Engineering and Mathematics (STEM) fields. Instead of second and third generations following the upward mobility pattern demonstrated in European-origin groups, generational research on Latino attainment demonstrates a "ceiling" of blocked opportunity (Chapa, 1990; Gans, 1992). The national public-school system is producing Latino youth who do not identify with their ethnic culture, nor are they equipped to competently function in the United States (Valenzuela, 1999).

What is the school's role? Research shows that US-born Latinos are "neither inherently anti-school nor oppositional. They oppose a schooling process that disrespects them; they oppose not education but *schooling*" (Valenzuela, 1999, p. 5). Valenzuela provides a framework called subtractive schooling to represent the patterns of Latino immigrant achievement and successive generational (US-born Latinos) underachievement or failure in schools. This framework argues that conventional schooling is organized in ways that strip low-income youth, particularly Mexican and Mexican American youth, of significant social and cultural resources (Jay, 2003; Urrieta, 2005; Valenzuela, 2003). This includes language discrimination and repressive schooling practices that make limited connections to

12

students' experiences and interests and that are characterized by worksheets and recitation (Murillo & Schall, 2016). This can even happen in school communities that claim to value bilingualism and student diversity when instructional practices do not reflect such claims (Garza & Crawford, 2005). Unfortunately, this progressive subtraction leaves Latino students increasingly susceptible to educational failure. This less than ideal consequence is exacerbated by a striking characteristic found in typical relationships between Latino students and their teachers—inauthentic connections and hostility (Valenzuela, 1997).

## TEACHERS

Why is there such distance between classroom teachers and their Latino students? For starters, there are differences in race, culture, and ethnicity. Looking at teacher demographics in 2016, White teachers make up 82 percent of the 3.3 million public-school teachers in the nation's PK–12 teaching force (USDE, 2016). This percentage is in sharp contrast to the 49 percent nonwhite students of the 50.1 million public-school students (USDE, 2016).

Historically, teaching and teacher education has been a field predominantly led by white individuals. Preservice teachers are often taught by white teacher educators (Talbert-Johnson & Tillman, 1999), and although more diverse teachers are being recruited into the profession, they leave at high rates[2], resulting in a public-school teacher workforce that is still mostly white (NCES, 2013).

---

[2] Overall, teachers of color are more likely to leave the profession than their White counterparts. However, teachers of color are more likely to work in hard-to-staff, urban schools that serve higher percentages of students of color and students from low-income homes, and experience conditions that undermine their retention—low levels of financial, human, and social capital, and lack of administrative support, teacher classroom autonomy, and teacher involvement in decision making. However, despite these conditions, teachers of color are more likely to remain in these schools than White teachers. What does drive teachers of color out of the profession are schools that lack multicultural capital—low expectations for students of color, lack of support for culturally sustaining or socially just teaching, and limited dialogue about race and equity (Achinstein, Ogawa, Sexton, & Freitas, 2010).

In contrast, our country is growing more diverse, and our classrooms reflect that change. The population that fills public-school classrooms is increasingly made up of children of color and Hispanic origins (Center for Public Education, 2013). Although it is not necessary for teachers to be of the same ethnic and racial background as their students to be successful at their job, this cultural, racial, and language mismatch may pose challenges to teachers' cultural awareness, understanding, and even the addressing of racism, prejudice, and the experiences of marginalized groups. It can often be a hurdle for students to use teachers as role models if they cannot identify with them in some form or another. It is critical that communities, educators, and policy makers confront and dismantle the academic barriers that Latinos encounter in the public-school system. As our nation becomes more and more diverse, our future rests on how well schools respond to educating Latinos.

# CHAPTER 2
# LEARNING TO DANCE AT HOME

*If you really want to make a friend, go to someone's house and eat with him…The people who give you their food give you their heart.*

~Cesar Chavez~

American farm worker, labor leader, civil rights activist, and
co-founder of the National Farm Workers Association

For most individuals, the very fibers of our identity can be traced back to home—the place we identify as a place of familiarity, love, security, and warmth. Home is more than just a house: home can be family and community. Home can be traditions or how we interact with others. Home can also be represented by single or multiple feelings, memories, and experiences.

## THE LATINO HOME

Culture often dictates home life, family context, and the ways in which communities and neighborhoods exist. Family is hugely important to the Latino community and is vital for understanding the lives of Latino students. Latino families tend to be larger than White, African American, and Asian families, with an average of five members per household (US Census Bureau, 2001). The national average is 2.58 (US Census Bureau, 2010). Why do Latino families tend to be larger?

There are a number of reasons. One reason for large households is due to the greater average number of children in Latino families. Another reason is that Latino households are more likely to be composed of extended family members. Nearly 6–10 percent of Latino homes include extended family members, compared to 3 percent in US households (Grau, Azmitia, & Quattlebaum, 2009). Due to higher rates of Latino poverty (20 percent vs. the US average of 9 percent), Latinos oftentimes rely on family for social and economic support by sharing living space. Finally, Latina teenagers have the highest birth rates of any racial and ethnic group (83 per 1,000 compared to the national average of 43 per 1,000) and the majority of these teen mothers live with their families (Population Resource Center, 2004). All of these trends are not surprising if you take into consideration the high value that the Latino community places on family (also known as familism).

Familism represents the emphasis placed on family and the importance of togetherness, solidarity, obligation, parental authority, and a high value on the needs of family over the needs of individuals (Cauce & Domenech-Rodriguez, 2002; Vega, 1995). For students, their responsibility and obligation to home may be a source of pride. For example, students may be delighted to show brothers and sisters their schoolwork, where they sit in the classroom, and what they do at school. Sharing family with school and vice versa may be a significant source of comfort for Latino students and their families. Furthermore, it is important to consider that for Latino students family may consist of *abuelas* (grandmothers), *abuleos* (grandfathers), *tios* (uncles), *tias* (aunts), and *primos* (cousins), and these individuals are much more likely to share childcare duties with the biological parent than in non-Latino families. Family, however, may simultaneously be a source of conflict. For example, as students prepare for their futures, attending college may challenge students' culturally embedded value of familism, particularly if it requires them to be away from home. This is not to say that Latino families do not value school. On the contrary, Latino parents have been shown to value academic success equally and social success more strongly than White parents (Ryan et al., 2010).

Where the Latino culture values familism, the American culture emphasizes individualism. This places Latino students in a precarious position, often forcing a choice between the two cultures. Walking the bicultural tightrope is particularly difficult for students if older family figures do not approve, because of another Latino value, *respeto* (respect). In Latino families this value represents a strongly held belief in the high regard for figures of authority, particularly elders. These values also resonate in the manners and behavior patterns of Latino children. In classrooms, Latino students may demonstrate respeto for the teacher with a quiet demeanor or waiting to engage in materials until directed so by an adult. Rather than interpreting this behavior as a sign of respect, the teacher might think the student is unmotivated, disengaged, or even disrespectful.

Because of their close-knit ties with family, Latino students may be particularly responsive to instruction and learning opportunities in classrooms that build community and allow them to work with others. Peer interaction and collaborative work are particularly important for building trust, or *confianza*, a very important value in the Latino culture (Souto-Manning, 2009). Establishing this confianza is particularly difficult for non-Latino teachers to forge with middle-school migrant students (Irizarry & Williams, 2013). Another prominent value that resonates in the parenting practices of Latino families is *bien educado* (well mannered), the importance of a good and moral upbringing (Reese et al., 1995). It may not be surprising that the Latino values of respeto and *educación* (education) often result in Latino parents' emphasis on self-control, obedience (Julian, McKenry, & McKelvey 1994), and conformity (Okagaki & Frensch, 1998).

Latino parents embrace a set of principles that emphasize mutual responsibility, sharing (e.g., interdependence; Harrison et al., 1990), and getting along with others (Julian et al., 1994), preparing children to function well in environments that value familism. Although there are differences within Latino cultures, both Puerto Rican- and Mexican-heritage mothers tend to be more controlling with their children than European American mothers, providing more physical guidance and structure within the home environment (Cardona, Nicholson, & Fox, 2000; Harwood et al., 1999; Ispa et al., 2004; Knight, Virdin, & Roosa, 1994). Latina mothers also tend to use more directive and nonverbal strategies (e.g., showing a child how to tie his or her shoe) and fewer verbal strategies (e.g., telling or asking a child about what steps need to be taken in order to tie his or her shoe) than White mothers (Laosa, 1978; Scholmerich et al., 1997). Latinos' values of control and respect are much more prevalent in Latino homes where there has been limited acculturation or adaptation to the dominant culture (e.g., American culture), and in homes of recent immigrants. Interestingly, and as found in other non-White groups, the use of control does not result in negative child outcomes as has been found in White homes (García Coll, Meyer, & Brillon, 1995; Jambunathan, Burts, & Pierce, 2000).

## CULTURE AND VALUES

As illustrated above, often the preferred child qualities in Mexican and Puerto Rican heritage homes clash with the American values that are promoted and rewarded in schools. For example, Mexican American and Puerto Rican heritage mothers place a greater emphasis on proper demeanor (e.g., appropriate behavior with others, role obligations) than self-maximization (e.g., individual potential, self-sufficiency), a belief system rated highly by European American mothers and valued in US schools. Clashes between these belief systems are clearly evident in educational patterns at home and at school. In Latino homes, the preferred educational interactions involve collaboration, support from siblings, and assistance with homework. In US classrooms that serve Hispanic students, direct instruction is often the model of choice. Students spend their time doing seatwork and being involved in whole-class discussion that includes drill and is led by the teacher (Padrón & Waxman, 1993)—a stark contrast to the ways in which these students learn at home. In a classroom where a White teacher might focus on individual student progress or foster a spirit of competition for personal achievement, the Latino students would be more receptive to practices that honor work that contributes to the success of the entire classroom, such as collaborative learning (see Padrón & Waxman, 1995 for other effective teaching practices for Latino students).

In summary, the primarily White teaching workforce present in the United States may inadvertently model more European American conceptualizations of parenting through instructional practices, whereas Latino students may be accustomed to different ways of learning from their home experiences. For teachers, it is vital to establish a greater awareness of what these home-school gaps can mean, particularly for Latino students' comfort level in the classroom, sense of belonging, and learning.

In the following essay, Elena García Ansani uses home as a lens for exploring the cultural missteps that have taken place in the lives of Latinos throughout history both inside and outside of school. This essay addresses how explicit or implicit forms of racism, discrimination, and oppression can quickly intrude at home, a place that is often characterized as nonthreatening, welcoming, and safe. Home may be where cultural missteps hurt the most because they shake the core of identity—something that is often intertwined with conceptualizations of home, particularly for students of color.

In greater detail, García Ansani presents the historical context of the cultural and racial discrimination that flourished in the 1960s. Of the civic struggles during the 1960s–1970s, the most widely recognized were the racial tensions between Blacks and Whites. Playing an equally important role, albeit less studied in history, were the Latinos in the Chicano Movement. The Chicano Movement, also known as *El Movimiento*, tackled broad issues of land grants, farm-workers' rights, enhanced education, voting, and political rights for Mexican Americans. García Ansani illustrates how these historical and very personal experiences shaped her development as a Latina.

CRITICAL THINKING—WARM-UP STRETCH: Think of a time in your life when the color of your skin played a role in how you were treated by a complete stranger—either negatively or positively. If positive, you may have experienced immediate acceptance into the context, for no apparent reason. Because there was little or no resistance in your admission to a group, conversation, or public setting, you may have a difficult time recalling this type of situation. If the event was negative, however, the experience will more quickly come to mind. Skin color may lead to rejection by a stranger when entering a store and being followed by the security agent. In conversation, it may be subtly evident in guarded body language and small talk. At the stranger's response, recall your feelings. Did you feel like you belonged? Good about yourself? Safe? Confident?

Now replay the scenario in your mind, but this time your skin color is different. Did the stranger respond to you differently? Have your feelings changed? What feelings stand out the most to you under this new circumstance?

## A Latina Journey of Empowerment

by Elena García Ansani

*Growing up during the '60s and '70s was a radical time of social unrest in American history. So many extraordinary events took place during those decades: the Civil Rights Movement, Vietnam War, Cuban missile crisis, arrival of the Rolling Stones and the Beatles, assassinations of JFK, Martin Luther King, Bobby Kennedy, and John Lennon, and space exploration landing the first men on the moon all made life-long lasting impressions on me. I look back at that era and also make note of the beginning of this country's determination to begin the deconstruction of systemic, historical racist policies, practices, attitudes, and ideologies deeply rooted in the infrastructure of the United States. It was a time to make way for the ushering in of antidiscrimination laws that would change the country unlike ever before. It's hard for young people today to believe that only fifty years ago, legal discrimination was rampant in this country. The riots during the 1968 Democratic Convention in*

*Chicago speak volumes to the civil unrest that existed during that era and serve as a reminder to me about the volatile undercurrents that existed between White dominant groups backed by forces of authority and those minority members of society who dared to challenge the ruling systems of power.*

*My memories of being harshly treated in discriminatory ways during those years still sting when I reflect about my educational experiences and recall certain teachers who doled out physical, verbal, mental, and emotional abuse regularly to Latino children for reasons I will never truly understand. Today, I know my Latina journey had to be what it was for me so that I could learn what I needed to learn and grow stronger along the way to be the Latina I was always meant to be.*

### *Little Village/La Villita*

*The tales of discrimination my parents experienced before they had any children were horrifying: police harassment because my dad spoke little English, landlords who wouldn't rent to them or evicted them once they learned they were Mexican, and other forms of humiliation in their workplaces, which ranged from denigrating ethnic epithets (i.e., spic, wetback, dirty Mexican) to the exploitation of them as workers who were not compensated fairly. Still, my family was one of the first Mexican families to buy a home in 1966 on the block I grew up on in Chicago's Little Village neighborhood. Back then, the neighborhood was 98 percent White. Today, young people familiar with the community will often express looks of incredulity when I've shared details with them about what it was like for me as a young child. The neighborhood was named Little Village during the early part of the twentieth century by central European immigrants from Czechoslovakia, Poland, and Germany who sought to create a Bohemian community similar in origin to what they were familiar with in their old country. I remember the manicured lawns, trimmed hedges, front-yard and backyard flower gardens, cars parked in garages overnight rather than on the street, penny-candy stores, the business district of Twenty-Sixth Street being relatively quiet except during the Fourth of July parade, riding the escalators and elevators in the Goldblatt's Department Store, buying school clothes from the Zemsky Brothers Store, the smells inside Polish bakeries, the long lines at the A&P food market, not understanding the European foreign languages being spoken by white people in most stores or in the advertisements they posted in their windows, and riding the Blue Island #60 bus all the way to downtown Chicago.*

**CRITICAL THINKING**: Regardless of immigrant status or language, the color of skin seems to be a dominant way individuals make assumptions about status. However, individuals who have white skin have endured discrimination from the American-born, native-English-speaking majority. For example, in earlier waves of immigration, Polish and Italian immigrants faced much discrimination. How are current immigration movements different or similar than those of the past? How are the situations of Latinos different or similar?

*By the early seventies, an escalated exodus of White flight had ensued where the majority of White inhabitants who once cherished Little Village were abandoning the community for suburbia. This transition ushered in La Villita and what would become one of the largest Latino communities in the Chicago area. By the early eighties, the sights, sounds, and landscape of the Twenty-Sixth Street area had been completely transformed. A vibrant Latino hub had emerged, filled with supermercados (supermarkets), specialty tiendas (stores) with everything from furniture to cowboy boots, tortilla factories, Mexican restaurants on almost every street from Kedzie to Pulaski, panaderias (bakeries) filling the air with heavenly scents, street vendors selling tasty treats of palletas de helado (popsicles), fresh fruit, elotes (corn), and tamales, along with loud Mexican music blaring from cars and homes. I experienced all these changes occurring in my community during my adolescent years. I often wonder how my life would have been different if Little Village was already La Villita when I was growing up. Because by the time I had graduated from high school, I felt like I had walked through fire.*

**CRITICAL THINKING**: How would you describe your childhood home? How might the author's life have been different (for better or worse) if La Villita existed during her childhood?

## School Years

*My siblings and I attended Catholic elementary and high school because my parents always believed that parochial education was the key to a better life. My parents earned a modest living to support our family of six. My dad worked as a factory-machine operator, and my mother held various office clerical positions. Yet, despite our humble means, my parents insisted on sending us to parochial schools because they wanted us to receive the best education they could provide us with despite the cost of tuition for four children. They believed their personal sacrifices were laying a strong foundation for our futures.*

*I think they also feared sending us to the nearby public schools where integration was being implemented due to the mandates of the Civil Rights Act of 1964, which outlawed major forms of discrimination against African Americans and women. Adults regularly protested outside these public schools with signs, name-calling, and other forms of harassment toward the minority children in attendance there. They would shout, "We were here first" and "No Negroes wanted here" or worse, spit on the children. I still cringe whenever I see video footage of that era and the faces of the white women and men who were protesting and their contorted expressions of rage but also fear.*

CRITICAL THINKING: Are these protests that the author describes different from or similar to the protests of today (i.e., immigration)?

*At the tender age of five, in kindergarten, I experienced my first taste of the contempt some White people had for Mexicans. Today, I know that these teachers, parents, and children were victims of their own blind ignorance and lack of cultural awareness, but when you are a young child and have an adult scream in your face to, "Go back to where you came from," I honestly thought I needed to go home. What they meant was that I should go back to Mexico. I did not understand this because I was born in this country. When I told my mother, she began to cry and told me it was because I was Mexican these people were saying these awful things to me. I really didn't understand what she was telling me. Why would teachers and other adults want to frighten a child? If their goal was to intimidate me...it worked. I had no idea what it meant to be a Mexican, but now I knew I was one. I often asked myself, what's wrong with being Mexican? What else could a young child think? A mental note was made at that early point in my life about being different.*

BACKGROUND KNOWLEDGE: As evidenced in this example, we know that children and adults internalize identity and race differently. Children construct attitudes about people who are unlike them by adopting social norms (as demonstrated in the home, media, school, and community) as well as through interactions with others. Children also form these ideas absent of direct interaction with individuals of different ethnic and racial backgrounds. As early as preschool, students display misconceptions about people who are different from themselves (Derman-Sparks & Ramsey, 2006).

*I looked in the mirror and saw a young girl…what did others see? When my teachers let me know my first and last names, Elena García, were not considered American by their standards, I had to question if it was really because of my ethnicity that I was treated in such a cruel, discriminatory manner throughout my school years. Looking back in retrospect, I know I learned to suppress my emotions during school to mask the hurt I felt from teachers who made me feel insignificant. My innocence was replaced by fear and mistrust. I became an introvert by default. In the safe confines of my mind, where my private thoughts and ongoing internal self-talk could question everything and everyone without repercussions, I was never oppressed there. In reality, it would take several decades for me to harness the courage to become the Latina I am today.*

*Since my brother was the oldest child in our family, he led the way at the school we attended. From kindergarten through eighth grade, he earned a reputation as a "troublemaker" mostly because he couldn't keep still during class. He was repeatedly punished and slapped in the face all through his elementary-school years by his teachers. As he was two grades ahead of me, and most of his teachers were my teachers when I entered the next grade after him, many of my teachers exhibited a contemptuous bias toward me from the beginning of the school year. I was called "García" more often than by my first name because my first name was often mangled by teachers and students who called me Ellen, Elaine, Alana, Eleanor, Eileen,*

*Helen. When I attempted to point out the correct pronunciation of Elena, I was dismissed, laughed at, or worse, ignored.*

**CLASSROOM CONNECTION**: A student who is suppressing emotions, reactions, and thoughts during the school day may appear withdrawn and/or noncommunicative by others whose experiences preclude the need to suppress natural responses and/or curiosities.

How can this behavior be misinterpreted by classroom teachers? Peers? How can this behavior impact student learning?

*One of my most confounding school memories occurred when I was a young child during second grade. My teacher (a European spinster, whose name was a variation of mine), Miss Alina, treated me in an awfully hostile manner for reasons I'm now certain were steeped in her racist attitudes. She often spoke to the other children in Polish. I remember on several occasions my classmates would turn to look at the few of us Latino children in the classroom and laugh after Miss Alina would say something in Polish. Miss Alina would always mock me for wanting to read aloud or answer a question. She often made remarks about me not being as smart as I thought I was. One day our class took a standardized reading test. After she had graded the tests, she accused me of cheating. I did not even know what she meant by the word cheating. I had taken the exam as I was instructed. She dragged me down to the principal's office by my braid and told her I had cheated on the reading test. She stated it was not possible for a Mexican child to score as high as I did on the reading test. The principal decided I would retake the test in the library under both their supervision. I retook the test and scored higher. I was reading at a sixth-grade level while I was in second grade. Miss Alina's protests that it could not be true were startling to me. Why couldn't it be true? Did she think Mexicans could not be smart? Miss Alina rarely acknowledged me after that incident. For the remainder of that school year, my teacher and fellow classmates treated me as if I was invisible. That was an emotionally painful experience, especially as this treatment would repeat itself time and again throughout my school years. It was during this time that I learned to cope with the stress of discrimination by deeply burying the deep emotional wounds I had endured during that stage of my life.*

*Because I was excluded during classroom discussions and ridiculed for asking and answering questions, I began to journal as a way to make sense of my world. As my identity was regularly diminished by teachers during my early school years, I developed a tough exterior to shield myself from the verbal, physical, psychological, and emotional attacks targeted against me by people I should have been able to trust but couldn't unless it meant accepting their label of worthlessness.*

*Writing, to me, about my life was a way of recording my experiences, but more importantly, it was a way for me to identify the social injustices that were commonplace in my world. My stories were not unique to me, as most of the Latino children at my school were treated similarly. Discrimination was part of our lives, and our obvious cultural, language, and physical differences were the triggers that led to our being ignored and treated as if we were invisible outsiders or worse, by being mocked and ridiculed both inside and outside our classrooms. Going to our school was not easy during the transitional changes taking place in Little Village/La Villita. The white teachers and students were angry that Latinos would soon become the majority population of the community. Throughout these years, I was told repeatedly I wasn't smart, despite being a straight-A student, nor should I plan on going to college because Mexicans didn't go to college. Being fiercely independent, I sought to find my answers for understanding my existence on my own. Today, I attribute my astute powers of observation and introspective analysis to those formative years of being witness to the injustices and oppression of minority people and everything else going on around me that was just plain wrong. During those years, I witnessed the people in my life to have the most power to be teachers. They could choose to treat us with the same respect and consideration as our fellow white classmates or not.*

**CLASSROOM CONNECTION**: Hurtful classroom practices and behaviors still exist today—many times delivered by well-meaning teachers who are simply unaware of the cultural experience of their students. For example, a teacher might easily misinterpret a student's quiet or guarded manner in the classroom as a symbol of the student's disinterest or rebellion, when as we learned earlier, it may simply be a student's learned protective mechanism.

In what ways can teachers appropriately use their power to eliminate racism and discrimination? How can teachers create a classroom environment that is intellectually challenging and safe for all?

*While growing up, movies and books were very important to me because they provided a way for me to better understand myself and the world I was living in. When I was in high school, I saw the movie Network. The main character, Howard Beale, was a news anchorman who was about to get fired from his job due to low ratings until he had a live, on the air, rant and encouraged the nation to shout out their windows, "I'm mad as hell, and I'm not going to take this anymore!" That scene struck such a chord for me. After the movie, I stuck my head out the car window and shouted I was mad as hell, and I wasn't going to take being treated as a second-class citizen anymore. I was tired of being the invisible girl and angry about the way I had been treated by my teachers and others. Back then, I asked myself often why I had allowed myself to accept the treatment that was doled out to me and my Latino classmates. My fear of the repercussions I would receive from my teachers had suppressed me from speaking up to them. I knew it was time to break free from those chains and defend myself from their oppressive biases. I challenged myself to speak out and began to advocate for myself. I learned quickly that by opposing the majority opinions, I was creating uncomfortable confrontational scenarios with my teachers and other students. I was sent to the principal's office more times than I care to remember during high school because I would no longer accept being silenced. There was no turning back for me now, because I had found my voice and the courage to speak out against racism, injustice, and discrimination that oppressed people of color. Although my confidence and self-esteem had been ripped to shreds throughout my schooling, I was determined to follow my heart and use my life experiences to find the answers for what I needed to do with my life.*

**CLASSROOM CONNECTION**: How does media affect a child's identity development and learning? In what ways can teachers use media to support positive student perspectives and outlooks?

## Embracing Empowerment

I am the oldest daughter in my family and naturally assumed the role of mother's helper and "teacher" when playing with my siblings. An avid reader by the age of five, I loved books and what I could learn from them. Reading was a way for me to escape and experience life in ways I didn't know existed. I learned to be a good student during my school years despite the lack of encouragement my teachers failed to provide. I wanted to prove everyone wrong who ever said to me that Mexicans weren't smart. I think there was also a fear of failure that ran deep inside of me, which compelled me to be driven to learn as much as I could inside and outside of school. Looking back, I have often questioned what was really driving me during those days. I honestly never enjoyed going to school because it wasn't fun or a positive environment for me in any way. When I close my eyes and remember those early years, I always go back to 1968 and a life-changing event that deeply affected who I was and who I am today.

Each summer during the first two weeks of July, my family drove from Chicago to San Luis Potosi, Mexico. Six of us in a car for hours on end without air conditioning was far from fun. We drove straight through, a twenty-four-hour drive, from Chicago to Houston, Texas. We stayed with my aunt for a few days and then packed up to drive another twenty-four hours to my dad's hometown in central Mexico. The summer I turned seven years old, we had a terrible car accident as we were heading back to the United States. There had been torrential rainstorms during our entire visit. Flooding and roads being washed out had occurred throughout Mexico. Although it was the middle of the night, I could never sleep during those road trips and was wide awake when I saw a man trying to flag my father down to stop. Our car was traveling well over sixty miles per hour. Everything happened so fast. My mother screamed, and our car plunged into a steep ravine caused by the road being washed away. Our car nose-dived and was precariously perched in a forty-five-degree angled position, back wheels barely gripping what was left of the road, while the front was immersed in water. It was a terrifying experience. My dad had hit his head on impact and was bleeding, my sisters were crying, my older brother was yelling, "WE NEED TO GET OUT," while my mother was screaming hysterically. I was in shock and felt like I was watching everything happen in slow motion. Suddenly, two men appeared and were pulling us out of the car. Within minutes of being out of the car, another car came barreling along and

28

careened off the road. It spun out of control and landed upside down in the water in its attempt to not crash into our car. In 1968, none of us had a cell phone or any way to call for emergency assistance. We were at least one hundred miles from the nearest town in the middle of nowhere, with no lights except for the stars above. The strangers who had appeared to help all of us were mysteriously gone…nowhere to be found. Shortly thereafter, a pickup truck came along and drove us all back to the nearest town. Miraculously, each of us had survived this harrowing ordeal, including the passengers in the second vehicle that was laying in the ravine like a turtle flipped on its shell.

I have been asked many times to share how I have been able to remain so positive and strong despite all the trials and tribulations that have presented themselves to me on my arduous life's journey. I find my resiliency is deeply connected to my recollection of that night on a lonely, dark, Mexican road, which is still very vivid for me even though it's more than forty years later. I knew then as I do today, we were more than fortunate to have survived that night. As a young child, I could not associate any sort of deep significance with my near-death experience. I know my parents' staunch religious beliefs as devout Catholics greatly influenced me then to believe we survived because we were protected by God. What I have held onto in my heart and mind ever since that night was that I was truly blessed and that I was on this planet for a reason. I could not tell you then or for many years thereafter, what my purpose for being here was. I only knew that I had survived and was alive. Something was different about me, though. I had obtained a heightened awareness about my existence. My parents can attest that I was always known to have a strong will, but I think I can trace back to that summer when I began to grow stronger in my convictions about the world I knew. Though it was not always easy for me to hold steadfast to what I knew to be right, wrong, true, false, good, or bad, especially when so much in my life was a contradiction of what it purported to be. Still, at the age of seven, I began to understand my life was important. Holding onto that simple fact through all of my life's challenges has helped me to always get up every time life has knocked me down. It would become clearer many years later that all my experiences with racism and discrimination were preparing me for the future. I had to be a strong Latina to be able to do the challenging work of advocating for social justice to empower myself so that I could be a guide for others who were also seeking to embrace their personal power and purpose.

**CLASSROOM CONNECTION**: Elena's confrontations with racism impacted her life perspective. What does that mean for teachers of Latino children? How can teachers support Latino empowerment and work for social justice in their relationships in the classroom, school, community, and world?

### *My Latina Journey*

*My Latina journey has certainly been full of tests of character and integrity at every stage of my life and has yet to cease. When I joined the workforce during the 1980s, unfortunately the stereotyping and ridiculing of my ethnicity had not ended. I can recall incidents where I was treated markedly differently by the White majority group at many of my employment places after I shared information about my ethnicity. At one job, a group of women was taunting and mocking a younger woman because she was speaking Spanish on the job. They would ask her if her back was wet and then laugh. Because I spoke up on her behalf and stated I did not agree with their perspectives of a "joke," I was forever shunned by the group. It became a repeated life lesson for many years, where coworkers would exclude me once they learned I was not really one of them. I did not intentionally want to have confrontations, but I refused to go along with a group who was putting down anyone because of their differences just so I could be accepted by their terms.*

*I still encounter people in many arenas who are oblivious to their blatant racist attitudes toward people of color. Sometimes during casual conversation, someone will still have the audacity to make an inappropriate comment to me about Latinos, ignorant that I am a Latina and part of the group they are putting down. Of course, I have to set them straight for the record, but it does get old. Fortunately, most people today will think twice before they say or do something in the workplace that could result in a discrimination lawsuit. What is most different about my interactions with others when these digressions occur is that the words no longer hurt. I know who I am and why I am. No one will ever have the power to negatively affect my self-esteem because I am a Mexican. I am proud to be a Latina of Mexican heritage. I enjoy sharing my culture with others. Occasionally, I am still asked what part of Mexico I was born in. I do love the look of incredulity in someone's eyes when I answer, "Berwyn, IL." If someone said to me they were Irish,*

*I wouldn't ask them what part of Ireland they are from. Now, this might sound silly to someone who is not a Latino. I've observed many interactions between White Americans and have noted they don't ask this question among themselves because there is no need to confirm that another White individual is as American as they are. I've witnessed this question only being asked by a White person to another white person when there was evidence of a European foreign accent from one of the parties. Why does this matter to White people?*

*These assumptions are not always afforded to Latinos with or without accents. At times, I felt like I was being interrogated about my identity by certain individuals who had the power to either affirm or disaffirm my right to be a member of a collective group. Because racism and discrimination still exist along with the negative stigmas many individuals associate with Mexicans (i.e., enter the United States illegally to steal jobs from Americans, criminals, uneducated, high-school dropouts, etc.), I work diligently to continue to remove the barriers that still exclude many Latinos.*

**CLASSROOM CONNECTION**: What does this mean for teachers? Can asking an individual about their country of origin be interpreted as questioning their citizenship or their rights?

Is there a better way to express interest in another's culture, language, and experience than asking them about their country of origin?

*White power continues to be a dominant force in many of the arenas I traverse. It is very disheartening for me to acknowledge that my greatest oppressors throughout my educational experiences and beyond have often been white women. I have questioned this a great deal throughout my life. As a feminist woman and educator advocate, I do not discriminate in the support I afford to others who have often been marginalized by the hegemony of various institutions. Surprisingly, women who've had the power to open a door to facilitate an act of inclusion on my behalf within a mutual social circle (i.e., classroom community, department meetings, team projects, and social gatherings) more often than not chose to limit my participation by not including me. I've learned how to break through these social barriers of exclusion but still wonder why the resistance to allow my entry persists.*

*Why I have not had the opportunities throughout my life that were naturally extended to my White counterparts (i.e., guidance in the college application process, encouraged to participate in extracurricular activities, invited to attend departmental professional development events, and included in work group events) is complex to understand. However, it is these experiences, from my early years as a child to an adult woman, that have propelled me to learn how to move from being on the outside to rightfully participating in all the groups I am a member of. When family members, friends, neighbors, students, teachers, or fellow committee members have sought my assistance for whatever the need be (i.e., guidance to gain equitable access to health services, educational support, or information about how to navigate bureaucratic systems), I have always done whatever I could to help someone move forward in their life's journey. How could I not?*

*How did I manage to become so resilient to the adversity I have experienced throughout my life? I know the only answer to be true for me is that I am empowered by God. My life has been a challenge every step of the way because of who I am. When I look in the mirror, I see a woman who is true to herself and others. I see a mujer (woman) who is strong and bold and tries every day to walk the walk and talk the talk about the work I need to do as a mother, wife, and scholar. I know I've learned from all my life experiences, good and bad. I have been strengthened by them to become the Latina I am today and more importantly to do all that I need to do as an empowered Latina.*

**About the author:** Dr. Elena García Ansani is a first-generation, nontraditional college graduate. She works as a College Access, Equity and Success consultant, research practitioner, and motivational speaker. Email: elena@egarciaansani.com

# Take It to the Classroom:

## Battling Racism

In this essay, the author provides an illustration of empowerment—how adversity was used as a catalyst to break a system of oppression. For many, however, the outcome is not nearly as positive, and these blatant or masked messages of discrimination and recycling of negative stereotypes threaten the hearts and homes of Latinos every day. Understanding and unpacking the experiences of minoritized groups becomes even more vital for the educational community, particularly as more than one in every four (27.4 percent) public-school elementary students is Latino. As noted in Chapter 1, Latinos are the largest minority group (16.5 percent) enrolled in college; however, graduation rates of Latinos still remain low. This essay illuminates the challenges and hurdles that Latinos face every day, beginning at a young age, and have the potential to inform the ways in which Latinos are supported in their pursuit of success.

In her essay, Elena shared her personal struggle with disbelief, shame, and indignation at harsh treatment and careless slurs that were tossed around as casually as darts. This essay enabled us to experience and view racism through the eyes of a young child, an indignant adolescent, and finally a resilient adult. Through perseverance, Elena revealed character-defining events and foundational beliefs that shaped the way she thought about herself as a student and as an empowered individual. The ways that students experience belonging in the K–12 classroom plays a huge role on the levels at which they learn and achieve. To that end, teachers must wield the power they hold in the classroom with great care and sensitivity.

## DISCUSSING RACE AND RACISM IN THE CLASSROOM

Talk about it: Talking about the topic of race and racism is the first step in working toward social justice. Ask students to reflect/write about the ways race and culture have affected their lives. Reflection through writing can be guided by a number of prompts that help students approach ideas related to race at the surface level and then leads them into deeper reflection. These exercises also serve as a way to address students as individuals while simultaneously allowing teachers to avoid broad assumptions about race and culture. Example prompts:

- Reflect on a value that is meaningful to you.
- Describe your culture.
- Describe an experience when being a member of your race made you feel special.
- Describe a time when you were made to feel uncomfortable because of your race.

Classroom Climate: Avoid making assumptions about your students' experiences. Create a safe and inviting classroom atmosphere so that everybody can share, experience, and achieve their highest level of autonomy. Start each day with a community-building check-in and have students respond in small groups and then in whole groups. Make sure that every student is heard and valued. Topics for the check-in could be: last night's homework, how you are feeling today, or one thing in your life you would change. If time is running short, as it often does in schools, each student could share *one word* about how they are feeling about the day. The topics could ideally be anything—the value of the exercise is empowering each and every student, not necessarily the topic of the check-in.

Create an inclusive environment: Teachers should make sure that classroom novels, picture books, posters, toys, manipulatives, music, and other resources are diverse in terms of race, ethnicity, gender, age, social position, family situations, disabilities, and so on. This variety in representation will not only give heterogeneously mixed students a feeling of belonging and acceptance in the classroom, but it will also introduce students to unexplored perspectives in the community and world around them. If biased materials or situations remain visible in the classroom, school, or community, use them as opportunities to discuss bias with students. Children's literature featuring Latino protagonists is limited, but there are great treasures to be found that connect to the Latino experience through history, tradition, common experiences, and beautiful illustrations. A small bibliography of culturally relevant children's books that can be used with Latino elementary students (Oberg de La Garza, 2013) is below. It is important to note that, despite the fact that these picture books are identified at a grade level below fourth grade, they introduce thought-provoking concepts and values that should be explored by learners of all ages.

- Agra Deedy, C. (2007). *Martina the Beautiful Cockroach*. Atlanta, GA: Peachtree Publishers.
- Andrews-Goebel, N. (2002). *The Pot That Juan Built*. New York: Lee & Low Books.
- Beatty, P. (2000). *Lupita Mañana*. New York: Harpercollins Juvenile Books.
- Bunting, E. (1996). *Going Home*. New York: Harpercollins Juvenile Books.
- Cartaya, Pablo (2017). *The Epic Fail of Arturo Zamora*. New York: Viking.
- Medina, Juana (2016). *Juana & Lucas*. Sommerville, MA: Candlewick Press.
- Medina, Meg (2015). *Mango, Abuela, and Me*. Sommerville, MA: Candlewick Press.
- Soto, G. (1996). *Too Many Tamales*. New York: Puffin

Daily Practice: Avoid a "tourist approach" to multiculturalism that limits diversity to history months, foods, and special events. There is minimal value in schools' hype over "International Day" celebrations, when daily practices impose assimilation of a singular culture. Cultural days of celebration run the risk of trivializing culture and offer students a more superficial understanding of a concept that is much richer, more multifaceted, and dynamic (Sleeter, 2011).

Teachers should weave a reverence of culture, traditions, and experiences systematically and purposefully into the everyday life of the classroom.

Lead: Be a role model who is a leader and advocate for social justice. Strive to demonstrate respect for the knowledge, talents, and diversity of all people. One strategy would be to develop an area in the classroom where recent news articles are posted to help students explore social justice. Students can be guided in selecting a local issue of social injustice that is meaningful to them by writing a letter to a local elected official.

## INSTRUCTIONAL METHODOLOGY

Engaging students in classroom practices and activities that foster belonging in K–12 will play an important role in students' learning and achievement. Cooperative learning groups is a tool that stimulates academic growth through participation. Group work invites students to see beyond superficial barriers and explore attitudes, ideas, experiences, and beliefs of group members collectively pursuing a common goal. Engaging students in varied grouping opportunities provides opportunities to more deeply master new content and ideas, the dynamics of teamwork, and communication (Powell, Cantrell, & Adams, 2001). Students can be grouped differently according to different purposes.

- o *Leveled Ability Groups* organize students by achievement levels or academic strengths. This type of group is essential when engaging students in specialized, guided reading or math activities with books of varied levels. One major drawback to this type of grouping method is that students quickly recognize who are the higher- and lower-achieving groups and may associate negatively with the identification. Leveled ability grouping should be used sparingly.
- o *Social (Cooperative) Grouping* assigns a specific role to each student in the group (e.g. leader, presenter, recorder,

helper, etc.) in order to help them practice certain social skills.

o *Task Group members* compose a group based on their strengths in specific tasks (e.g., an artistically talented group of students designs scenery for a play).

o *Interest Groups* are organized by teachers or students themselves based on interests in a particular topic (e.g., rainforest ecosystems, baseball-team statistics, etc.).

o *Random Groups* are formed arbitrarily by counting off numbers or drawing cards. This type of grouping can be used to help students get to know each other and is used when focus is on management and forming groups of equal size.

o *Student Choice Groups.* It is good to occasionally allow students to form their own groups, with teacher supervision.

Other methods to authentically engage all students in eliminating racism through learning strategies incorporate varied, multisensory learning activities. Students can make posters promoting differences and individuality. Teachers can guide students through role-play scenarios. Using the writing process, students can create and perform raps, poems, and skits that reflect personal values or ideas. Classes can enjoy student-selected music during independent work time, or teachers can incorporate the music into expressive-movement activities. An experiential learning approach involves students in feeling the sting of discrimination through preferential treatment given to specific groups of students based on a specific eye color or right or left-handedness (see *Frontline*'s resources *A Class Divided* at http://www.pbs.org/wgbh/pages/frontline/shows/divided/). One simple activity that can provide a strong foundation in the acceptance of others is called When Life Hands You a Lemon, Peel It, which follows. This lesson can be adapted for students in grades K–12, to focus on the spectrum of perspectives based on diverse patterns of experiences.

For lesson plans that explore social justice issues, film kits, teaching strategies, printable posters, and other classroom resources, see www.tolerance.org (Teaching Tolerance).

**Classroom Activity: When Life Hands You a Lemon, Peel It**

This fifteen-minute activity aims to show children that despite outside differences, people are often similar on the inside.

Organize students into small groups and give one lemon to each child. Ask students to "get to know your lemon" through examination: smell them, touch them, throw them in the air, and roll them around. After a few minutes, give each group a paper bag and ask them to place lemons in the bag. Then, ask the children to empty the bags and find their lemons in the pile. Remarkably, most children will recognize their lemons at once. Some will even get protective of them. Next, ask the children to describe how they recognized their lemons.

"My lemon was big," one might say.

"My lemon had a mark on one side."

And another, "My lemon had dents and bruises."

Then talk about how people, too, come in different sizes, different shapes, different shades of color, and different "dents and bruises."

After exploring these ideas, ask students to peel the lemons and return them to the bag. Then ask the children to again find their lemons. Presented with this quandary, children will usually exclaim, "But the lemons all look the same!" This reaction opens the door to discussing how people, like lemons, are often similar on the inside.

This lesson can have a lasting impact, particularly if revisited when students are facing issues of conflict.

Adapted from *Talking to Your Child About Hatred and Prejudice* by C. M. Stern-LaRosa (Anti-Defamation League, 2001).

# CHAPTER 3: IDENTITY
# AND PERSONAL EXPERIENCES

*Equality, trust and love are essential in classrooms in order for education to be used as a means toward liberation and a disruption to the systemic hierarchy and power relationships between students and teachers.*

~Curtis Acosta~

High School educator in Tucson, AZ, developer of the Mexican American Studies program featured in the documentary *Precious Knowledge*

"Who are you?" This is the question that knocks on our door the moment we are born and returns to us throughout life. The age-old nature vs. nurture debate pins two influences against one another—is development (or in this case, identity) primarily driven by biological or environmental factors? It has been widely recognized that both nature and nurture influence an individual in important ways (DeFries, Plomin, & Fulker, 1994). In addition, these elements interact with one another in reciprocal ways (Bandura, 1989). For example, if I (Alyson Lavigne) was given a personality assessment, I would likely rate high on extraversion—I live for new opportunities and experiences, am active, like to be part of a group, and unfortunately for those around me, I like to talk a lot! So, how did this become such a large part of my personality? Could it be that I had access to lots of neighborhood kids as a child, my parents took me to regular social outings, and, therefore, I am outgoing? Or did I acquire my effervescence from my parents? And, therefore, engaged with neighborhood kids and in community outings in a way that reinforced my preexisting personality trait (e.g., I introduced myself to my peers and invited them to play rather than playing alone and isolating myself from the group)? Development is a result of what is termed *dynamic interactionism*—we are at the "same time both products of [our] social world and producers of it" (Lerner, 1978, p. 1).

This progression in developmental research has focused primarily on gene X environment interactions. A gene X environment interaction occurs when the effect of an environmental influence on particular outcomes (e.g., health and behavior) is dependent on genetics, or an environmental context moderates the effects of a given genotype on said outcomes. Many times, researchers have explored these interactions by studying individuals who possess a large amount of shared genetic material—twins. By comparing the outcomes of twins who lived in the same home (shared environment) to those who did not (nonshared environment; Cerda et al., 2010), researchers are able to make more precise conclusions about how genetic and environmental influences interact. This is captured most vividly by twins separated at birth and reunited later, who realize just how much they have in common (or not)—similar hairstyles, lifestyles, occupations, and timing of important life events such as marriage or birth of a first child (Schein & Bernstein, 2007). Twin studies have allowed for a better understanding of just how much biological and environmental factors shape particular parts of development.

As noted in Chapter 2, some of these environmental factors are cultural and help determine to what level we, as individuals, feel like we belong. Belongingness can be defined as relatedness or a desire to relate to and care for others and for others to do the same for oneself—an authentic involvement in one's social world (Deci & Ryan, 1991). Goodenow (1993, p. 80) argues that in the context of school, a sense of belonging is "the extent to which students feel personally accepted, respected, included, and supported by others in the school social environment." Students every day may face challenges of belongingness that are related to any one of many aspects of their identity.

## IDENTITY DEVELOPMENT

Teachers, understandably, focus their concern on environmental factors, particularly the types of experiences they can provide in their classroom that support the growth and development of all learners. Students enter the classroom with a number of experiences that have already begun to shape who they are and who they will become. This definition of self can encapsulate a number of elements: (a) our interests, beliefs, expectations, and values, (b) how we identify ourselves in terms of race, ethnicity, religion, sexual orientation, and social class, (c) physical identity (e.g., body image), (d) school and career achievement, and (e) political identity, to name a few.

Early in development, students frequently associate with the most concrete and apparent parts of identity—physical features that make them who they are, relationships with other people, and activities they are involved in on a frequent basis. I can run fast. I am tall. I like my teacher. I have brown hair. I like to read. My best friend is Janet. Later in development, students develop a richer understanding of identity—they hold beliefs, values, and particular personality and dispositional characteristics. For example, students begin to differentiate between ability, enjoyment, and interest in a given task or subject. They can assess to what extent others would want them as a friend (Marsh et al., 1984). They can reflect on how well they get along with others. They also challenge these self-ascriptions, trying them out in different settings and with different people.

## BELONGING AND OUTCOMES

Identity, a fidelity to yourself, and a feeling of belongingness, are critical for student learning. Oftentimes and unknowingly, identity is developed by our surroundings and the individuals in those surroundings. Expectations, stereotypes, and beliefs held by others can transform the beliefs we hold for ourselves and our behavior. This phenomenon is called the Pygmalion effect (Rosenthal & Jacobson, 1968). Essentially, a teacher's expectation for a student can become a self-fulfilling prophecy. For example, let us imagine that before getting a new class of third graders, a teacher is given the names of students who struggle with reading. The teacher, unknowingly, adjusts his or her instruction, expectations, and interactions with those students. The students, in turn, receive the message that they are not good readers, internalize this belief, and perform worse on reading tasks. Unfortunately, students use this information, in part, to establish whether or not they "belong" in the classroom and can perform the tasks required to be successful (as defined by culturally embedded constructions of success).

Belonging can organize around a number of factors including language, race, opinions, or beliefs that are not valued either directly (at home, by peers, or in the classroom) or indirectly (at a political and societal level). Belonging functions hand-in-hand with identity—for most individuals we want to feel accepted for who we are and feel we have a place in the world.

According to Maslow's early work (1943, 1954), individuals function within a hierarchy of needs that leads to self-actualization. The most basic needs for survival need to be met first (e.g., food and water), followed by safety. Once these needs have been acquired, an individual can focus on the need to belong—to feel accepted, and this often leads to fulfilling esteem needs—being recognized for potential and being rewarded for who you are and what you do. Self-actualization is at the top of the hierarchy, and this is fulfilling one's maximum potential. Recognizing this theory as a theory of motivation and applying this work to the classroom means that students need to have certain needs met in order to be their best—academically and otherwise. Identity and belongingness are part of that equation. The figure below organizes the five levels of need starting with the most basic needs at the bottom.

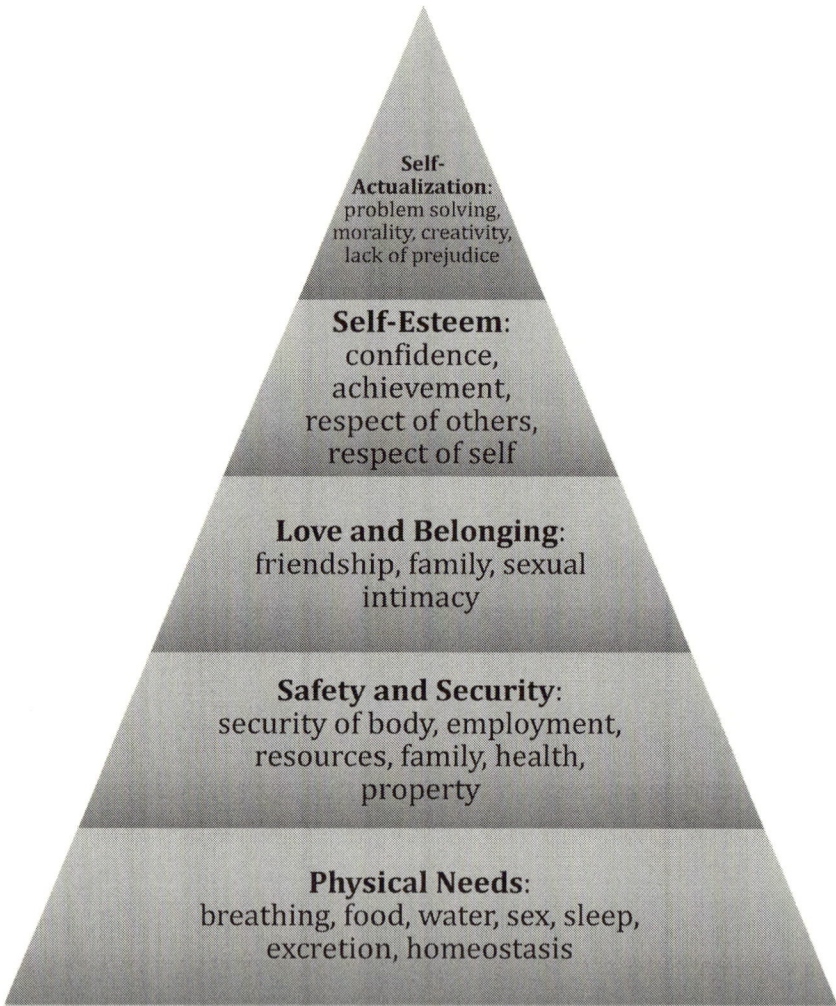

**Figure 3.1** *Maslow's Hierarchy of Needs*

More recent theorists have engaged belongingness in what they believe is a basic need that students need to establish for learning. According to Deci and Ryan (2000), relatedness (or a sense of belonging) is one major component of Self-Determination Theory— one model that seeks to explain students' intrinsic motivation. Students reported that feeling accepted by their teachers (relatedness) is associated with their engagement in the classroom (Furrer & Skinner, 2003). Furthermore, students who report caring and warm relationships with teachers display higher levels of intrinsic motivation (Ryan & Golnick, 1986; Ryan, Stiller, & Lynch, 1994). Hence, a sense of belonging is vital to students' success in the classroom.

Maintaining a sense of authentic identity and belonging for every student can be challenging. There are countless classroom situations in which teachers won't have sufficient time to plan for a carefully crafted response that will foster positive identity and a sense of belonging. To secure the safety of students, teachers must consider and explore personal underlying and unexplored assumptions, expectations, and experiences with other cultures. This next essay invites the reader to begin that exploration via a firsthand look into an unplanned classroom interaction that haunted one Latina for years. In the following narrative, Sarah Rafael García, a Mexican American ESL teacher, shares her own vivid trauma of being educated in a time "when there was no such thing as bilingual education" by well-intentioned but misguided teachers. García addresses her personal struggle with maintaining cultural pride after academically pushing her Spanish language into the background.

CRITICAL THINKING—WARM-UP STRETCH: Before reading this essay, think about one of your most cherished family traditions. What memories do you associate with it? What are the activities, foods, practices, sounds, and smells that are connected to this tradition? Now imagine something was preventing you from participating in this celebration with your family and friends. You look through a window and see your family gathered and enjoying themselves, but you are unable to open the window to join the festivities with them.

What thoughts race through your mind? How does that make you feel? What if you were told that you would have to sacrifice this sacred family tradition for a potential benefit for the future. Is anything worth this cost? If so, what?

## Ch-air, ch-air, chair!

### by Sarah Rafael García

*While teaching English as a second language in Beijing, China, at the age of thirty-one, I recalled my own childhood nightmares of learning English in elementary school. Those memories, combined with being immersed into my Mexican family's new culture in America, led me to reflect on the identity issues I encountered during my college years and develop my newly found cultural pride. It is not apparent through the daily words I use, but Spanish was my first language. For the first four years of my life, I lived near my grandparents who only spoke Spanish. I was completely surrounded by a proud Spanish-speaking environment in Brownsville, Texas. That all changed when my immediate family and I relocated to Orange County, California, in the late 1970s, when I was four years old.*

*I didn't really learn English until I started elementary school in the Garden Grove School District. While I was growing up, my mother would often remind me and declare to others that as a young child, I spoke perfect Spanish. I think the constant reminders as an insecure youth made me feel that my Spanish was not of a proud Mexican. I did not feel I was living up to my mother's Mexican standards. The humiliation was starting to diminish the little confidence I had as a child, not only as one of Mexican culture but also as an independent being.*

*The inherent shame of losing connection with my mother tongue led me to study Spanish throughout middle- and high-school years just to prove my cultural identity and pride. I even minored in Spanish during college. As I grew older, I began to seek acceptance from my own cultural group rather than approval from the US school system that had created societal expectations for me as a child. While at Southwest Texas State University in 1996, I tried to join a Mexican American social organization, but I was rejected because they didn't find me to be Mexican enough. Honestly, I'm not complaining about my experience. I benefitted from non-Mexican portrayal by building autonomous relationships that were not related to my culture or family; the experiences raised my confidence and exposed me to understanding the world outside of my cultural upbringing.*

*Being bilingual and culturally ambiguous opened many doors for me in the workplace before I had a degree. But it seems now, as an accomplished adult, I am trying to find a balance, maybe a better sense of personal acculturation, and acceptance from the identities I have accepted: Mexican American and bilingual. I definitely need to clarify and preface my story with the fact that I am quite empathetic toward anyone who has to learn English as a second language and still find a way to keep his or her family's native language and cultural pride while establishing themselves in an acceptable social status.*

**CRITICAL THINKING:** What are the consequences of assimilation? What does this change mean for Sarah outside of her family home? What was her motivation for studying Spanish in each of her levels of schooling?

How might students feel who are caught in between (e.g., not Mexican enough, yet not American enough)? "Being bilingual and culturally ambiguous" is a self-description that vulnerably reveals a huge distinction of identity lenses. If there is more to cultural identity than language, consider what other "elements" need to be present to form cultural identity? For support, consider your own identity—what elements of your character "define" who you are? Race? Gender? Career? Appearance? Relationships? Address?

*Both of my parents were sent to bilingual classes when they arrived in Texas in the late 1960s, when they were in their early teen years. The impact our societal system had on both of them was completely different, not just in their adaptation to the new language but also in their perception of social status. I realize now that my parents were protecting us by not letting us be placed in ESL (English as a Second Language) classes so that we wouldn't experience what they had.*

*Throughout my childhood, my father learned to accept the cultural change in his new country and practiced on a daily basis to improve his English and minimize his accent. I witnessed his various attempts to improve his English but never understood his intention until I myself was faced with creating my own identity. His efforts were more apparent to me after my own experience in fourth grade and throughout the rest of my education.*

**CLASSROOM CONNECTION:** Students learning English in the classroom may be facing inner turmoil about confidence and identity. Without programs in place to support formal native-language development, ELLs face disconnections between their native culture, familial ties, and rich values and traditions to varying degrees. Beyond superficial multicultural-awareness weeks that feature the four Fs— fairs, festivals, food, and folktales (Banks, 2002), how can classroom teachers support and foster connections to students' native language and heritage? What everyday practices can be in place across the curriculum? Instructional methodology? Classroom resources?

*I recall sitting around the dinner table practicing difficult words with him, especially when it came time for his reviews at work and interviews for a promotion. I can proudly say that he started in the pressroom as a janitor, and ten years later at the age of thirty-six, a month before he passed away, he not only received a head-supervisor position in the print room but was also naturalized as a US citizen. It was then that my father introduced me to the term Mexican American.*

*My mother, on the other hand, reprimanded us when we corrected her English as children. She felt we were being disrespectful and reminded us that we also spoke Spanish. Once we got older and still witnessed my mother making common mistakes such as pronouncing a neighbor's name as "Bicki" instead of*

*"Vicki" or an even more embarrassing moment for my youngest sister, Nydia, and her eleven-year-old classmates, when Mami suggested they eat at "Fuckruckers" instead of "Fudruckers." We asked her why she didn't make the effort to improve her English, especially since we lived in a predominantly "white" neighborhood. She then shared painful stories about her attempts to learn English as a second language in the American school system.*

*In her first year in the United States, she was susceptible to ridicule from her peers, including Mexican students who felt they were superior to her simply because they understood more English than she did. Her innate reaction was to reject the English language and hold on to her accent. She says her accent represents who she is and how she got to the United States of America. To this day, she has avoided obtaining her citizenship. She continues to fight against any form of assimilation and acquiring her American accent, but of course the combination of her circumstances has caused her to remain stagnated socially. During one discussion in her new home in Miami, my mother managed to impress me and enlighten my viewpoints on assimilation, but only after I criticized her by saying her accent had gotten worse since she moved to Miami.*

*She responded, saying, "What do you mean I have an accent? ¿Y qué importa? ¡El minuto que caminas afuera encuentras 'Americanos' que tienen acentos de todas partes del mundo! (Why does it matter? The minute you walk outside, you find 'Americans' who have accents from all over the world!) A todos se les olvida que sus padres también tenían acento cuando llegaron. (They all forget that their fathers also had an accent when they arrived.) Maybe they need to assimilate to OUR America, not me to theirs."*

*My mother will probably never admit to this, but her lack of English led her to miss out on education. The teaching methods combined with the ridicule instilled in her a feeling of insecurity in this new country, which only led her to drop out of high school and obtain a GED with no further higher education other than vocational training. I have to admit that I, as well as my sisters, sometimes think less of her and don't seek her opinion on some subjects due to her lack of education. I find that many people associate an accent or lack of English with the person not being knowledgeable or in many cases incapable. There are moments like the conversation that I mentioned that remind us of Mami's life experiences and her intellect, and now we proudly encourage her to return to school. Unfortunately, she still undermines herself by using her age as an excuse, but we never questioned her accent again.*

CRITICAL THINKING: Revisit your buried associations with people who have limited English or speak with an accent. Sarah reveals her mother's belief that limited-English speakers have limited intelligence. If a teacher carries unexplored biases or assumptions, what dangers can he or she pose to the educational outlook of a second-language learner in the classroom? Are you brave enough to explore your uncovered biases?

*I still remember vividly the times throughout my own childhood in which I was repeatedly corrected in class for pronouncing a word incorrectly or with an accent. In the late 1970s and early '80s, there was no such thing as bilingual classes for children in southern California, which in the long run, had advantages as well as disadvantages. Not only were teachers forced to "mainstream" children who had trouble with English pronunciation in with the "regular" students, but also their training didn't address this new dilemma within our society. To make matters more difficult, they did have an ESL class for bilingual students; however, it usually meant you were taken out of the regular class session to improve your English. It caused a greater disadvantage than being singled out in class and ran the risk of a student falling behind in studies and possibly not passing to the next grade.*

*During my first years in school, the new teachers asked me if English or Spanish was my first language. At the time, I didn't know the reason behind the question. I proudly answered, "Spanish!" That same day I was sent to ESL class, and a note was sent home to my parents. The next morning my parents accompanied me to school, and there was some kind of confrontation in which the teacher appeared angry when she was told by my parents in broken English that I would no longer attend ESL classes. Although I was relieved that I would no longer feel outcast in class, I now felt ashamed of my parents' English. This apparently happened to many bilingual students in our district; our neighborhood included various families of diverse backgrounds, but the majority of bilingual students were of Mexican, Samoan, and Vietnamese immigrants. Eventually my parents coached me to state that English was my first language. They did not want me or my sisters to face the ridicule and embarrassment they faced as new immigrants in the United States of America. The conversation of being forced to attend ESL classes was not only part of my family's immigrant experience, but it was a common conversation among the parents of my peers who included many Mexican, Samoan, and Vietnamese neighbors. My parents were very creative when explaining to me in Spanish that it was OK to lie to my teacher and state that English was my first language.*

CRITICAL THINKING: For what benefit would parents of English-Language Learners claim to be native-English speakers? How does it reflect the current political/educational/economic/social climate? Why would a school try to convince a family to accept or refuse bilingual classes for their child(ren)? In whose best interest is this decision? Why? How? What role does high-stakes testing play?

*I spent the first five years of elementary school trying to lose my Spanish and the accent that lingered when I spoke English. I began to lose my Mexican pride. At the time, I felt my language was my cultural pride and that the teachers didn't seem to like it because I pronounced everything wrong. Eventually this led me to assimilate with the American culture. At the time I was only a child who expressed this by feeling resentment and embarrassment. Unfortunately, the repercussions only got worse. We all began to speak English at home, which started to concern my parents and embarrass them when we would correct their English. A firm rule was set that we could not speak English at home, simply so we could practice our Spanish and hold on to our family's culture.*

CRITICAL THINKING: Whether intended or not, classroom teachers strongly influenced this author's fluency and attitude about her native language and culture. Sarah tried so hard to "fit in" that she rejected her Mexican culture and primary language in order to "assimilate with the American culture." Return to the warm-up activity at the beginning of this essay. If the cost of fitting in and being accepted by classroom teachers is the sacrifice of native culture and language, is it worth the expense?

*My parents were unaware of the constant turmoil I faced at school because of my limited English and inability to practice English at home. There were two different occasions in fourth grade in which I actually started to cry in class due to the learning method my teacher decided to implement. On the first occasion, I was asked to read the word "chair" out loud. I said what sounded like "share." I was then asked to stand up and repeat the word while facing the class. I repeatedly said it incorrectly. The teacher insisted that I could not return to my seat until the word was pronounced accurately. After numerous attempts, I could feel my eyes fill with tears, and there was an immense pressure in my chest. I started twiddling my fingers and stared at the ceiling instead of my classmates, who only expressed blank looks on their faces after my many attempts to say the word "ch-air." I got so frustrated with myself because each attempt sounded perfect in my head, but the sound never seemed to make it through my mouth. It was as if it got stuck somewhere between my Mexican pride and the voice of my blond teacher insisting that I needed to try again.*

*At some point, the pressure in my chest manifested to a hysterical cry that switched my focus from saying, "ch-air" to just being able to breathe. The teacher seemed remorseful and asked me quite nicely to return to my seat. She tried to continue with her lesson, but most students hesitated from participating, especially the Spanish-speaking and Vietnamese-speaking students. No one, not even the white kids, tried to be the teacher's pet that day. The lesson abruptly ended as we moved on to another subject.*

**CLASSROOM CONNECTION**: Consider the actions of the teacher on this day. What led her to employ this teaching method that haunted the student to present-day memories?

Jump into the shoes of the teacher. Try to tell this story from the perspective of the teacher. Complete the following sentence starters:

(a) The teacher didn't intend on hurting the student, she was really trying to…

(b) The message that the teacher was trying to send was…

*The next pronunciation "lesson" occurred during the week when it was our class's turn to put on a performance in front of the whole school. Of course, each student was expected to participate by speaking into a microphone in front of the entire campus. Even before my part was assigned to me, I was loathing the idea. Surely the teacher wasn't going to choose me. She couldn't, not with the accent I had. Apparently, she believed in the "equal opportunity" policy the school district implemented because, sure enough, I was chosen as the host speaker. I never understood why she insisted on making me speak. It was bad enough that I hated speaking English in front of my class since the whole "ch-air" incident, but now this same teacher wanted to further embarrass me by forcing me to speak to the entire student body. Not only was I supposed to introduce our class, but I also had to start out the presentation with "A is for…"*

*This time, the teacher decided to have the teacher's aide lead the rest of the lesson while she helped me practice the speech just outside the classroom door. I still managed to get frustrated and cry, but this time the teacher said, "Good job. Just try your best, and it will be all right, OK?"*

*I sniffled and said, "OK."*

*A couple of days later, I was standing in front of the entire school. Mami had done my hair with a big red bow. I was wearing my Sunday clothes but still felt very ugly and nervous. There were hundreds of students staring at me. OK, maybe not hundreds, but at the age of nine, thirty people felt like a hundred.*

CRITICAL THINKING: If you were a teacher in this school, would you oppose this type of ceremony or not? Do these activities include or exclude ESL learners? Both? In some cases the risk is very high— success can go a long way, but failure can be even more damaging.

*I took a deep breath and asked God to help me. I said a prayer in my head so I could talk to him in Spanish.*

*"OK, here it goes. Just try your best," my teacher said.*

*The microphone was turned on, so my deep breaths echoed out to the crowd. Teachers began to smile, and students were waiting for me to say something. As the words came out, I could hear them, not just in my head, but flowing perfectly toward the crowd, "A IS for…"*

*When it was time for me to walk away, I looked over to my blonde teacher, and I remember her winking at me. I knew I had done my best and that she accepted me. Whether her teaching techniques were appropriate or not, she was just doing her best, too. This was a new era in time for all of us. Things were changing. People were changing, and it was apparent different languages and cultural identities were surfacing into the school system.*

**CRITICAL THINKING**: Do these 1980s tensions still exist in current-day classroom interactions? Are they more veiled than they were several decades ago?

*Just like my parents had to find a way for me to receive a fair education and still manage to keep my first language, my teacher and I had to find a way to learn from each other and try our best. Together we all did just that—tried our best. Since then, all words in English and Spanish began to feel more natural. I can't remember what "A" is for because all I can recall is how to say "A" and "is" separately. I obviously had trouble with my speech. It was too difficult to separate "A" and "is." I would pronounce it as "As" or "Ass." I think it was due to nervousness. Even to this day, I still speak too fast, but my confidence has most definitely improved. Now, I'm told I speak too much in both English and Spanish. Muchas gracias (Many thanks) to my fourth-grade teacher!*

*Now, throughout the United States, numerous school districts have incorporated bilingual classes into the elementary schools. Bilingual classes are not just part of recent generations. This method was implemented in the United States when the first immigrants arrived, namely the Germans and the French. In addition, Texas used the same method for helping students from Mexico learn a second language. My sister Suzanne and I both chose to teach ESL and address bilingual education; I am currently an MFA student in route of a PhD in Education, and Suzanne is currently a PhD student in Education with an emphasis in bilingual studies. My youngest sister Nydia is also teaching her children Spanish and English while both sisters seek alternative education that aims to expose their children to our mother tongue and diverse cultures. We are all reaching to obtain a balance within our immediate lifestyle while transmitting the pride to the next generation. In lieu of all the stories that preceded my potential outcomes, I still aspire to embrace Spanish as a symbol of my Mexican culture and a sense of belonging in society.*

**CRITICAL THINKING**: Can language and culture be separated? What is an example of this?

*As I mentioned before, English as a second language in any "system" has both its advantages and disadvantages. Some of us have learned to assimilate into this new American culture, while others like myself (now at the age of thirty-eight) eventually discover that we can choose to acculturate instead and keep our initial pride. When I say "us," it's no longer just us Mexicans. "Us" is everyone in the United States, first, second, third, and all generations. Mexicans, Samoans, Vietnamese, Irish, Germans, Colombians, Afghanis, Persians, Jewish, Venezuelans, Chinese, and Japanese. We are all essentially American.*

*Although I do not feel I have mastered the English or Spanish languages in their entirety, I am confident I can communicate my cultural pride and sense of urgency to maintain it. The identity struggles still exist. Can I pronounce everything correctly in English and Spanish? Am I Mexican enough for my culture? Have I reached my full potential in this American society? I don't think there is one explanation that will ever answer all these questions. I am proud of who I am; the existence of my cultural pride is no longer dependent on what others question, accept, or how I pronounce the word "chair." It solely lies on what I choose to embrace. Because no matter what I say or how I say it, I am Mexican American, and Spanish is my first language.*

**About the author:** Sarah Rafael García is a Mexican American who speaks Spanish, English, and some Mandarin. Her parents and grandparents migrated from Matamoros Tamaulipas, Mexico, to Brownsville, Texas, in the 1960s. Sarah was born in the United States, the first US citizen on both sides of her family. She was raised in Austin, Texas, and currently lives in Santa Ana, California.

# Take It to the Classroom:

## Supporting Identity and Belonging

Elementary and high school teachers interact with hundreds, if not thousands of students over the span of a career. Despite careful planning, K–12 educators face unexpected situations that require rapid decisions on a daily basis. Sometimes the chosen direction leads to failure for a whole class, and sometimes the practice can be bad for a single student. For example, in research with Mexican-heritage students, Pease-Alvarez (2002) found that some students used language as a defense against being stripped of their culture and language.

> Roberto Fuentes, a thirteen-year-old child whose mother immigrated to this country as a child, told us (the researchers) how what he perceived to be his teacher's discriminatory treatment of Latinos had contributed to changes in his language preferences. According to Roberto, he preferred using English when he was younger. However, as he came into contact with teachers who reprimanded him and other Latino children when they used Spanish, he developed a preference for Spanish. In elaborating this viewpoint, he told us (the researchers) that now when he speaks with his teachers, "Les hablo en español para hacerles enojar—I speak to them in Spanish to make them mad." (p. 122).

From Sarah's account, the reader does not know if this situation was isolated or a regular occurrence in her teacher's repertoire. We get a clue when the teacher eases up and relents with, "Good job. Just try your best, and it will be all right, OK?" This offering reveals that the teacher most likely did not harbor ill will or intend to hurt Sarah so viscerally. Assuming that is the case, to prevent such harm from occurring in the classroom, it's important to examine the philosophies under which the teacher operated. Was it an expression of the teacher's high expectations for all her students? For

English Language Learners (ELLs)? Or Sarah in particular? Does the teacher espouse the value of hard work leads to success? Was the teacher demonstrating a firm commitment to her students' English proficiency, no matter the cost?

## BELONGING IN ANOTHER LANGUAGE

In Sarah's pursuit of learning English, she was pulled out of the classroom on a regular basis for English instruction. This method of pullout-ESL instruction is the most commonly practiced, and the least socially responsive model used today. Given that the ESL student spends less than 10 percent of the school day learning English, it would be logical to conclude that the student's classroom teacher will play a large role in supporting English learning. Caring for an ESL student's language development is not the only responsibility of a mainstream classroom teacher, however. Culture, motivation, identity, and self-esteem are also important parts of the whole education that the classroom teacher carefully manages in the course of every day and each academic year. In the past it was common for teachers to overlook the small handful of "those students" who sat quietly at desks struggling to navigate two languages and two identities. Those days are over. Today there are more than a handful of "those students," who aren't being served with as much care and resources as they deserve. With Latino students falling through the cracks and academically failing at epidemic rates, the time has come for change. Authentic change happens one teacher at a time. It starts with you.

At the climax of the essay, Sarah writes, "It was as if the pronunciation of the word 'chair' got stuck somewhere between my Mexican pride and the voice of my blonde teacher insisting that I needed to try again." This connotes tension between identity-challenged Latino students and well-intentioned teacher practices. What does this mean for Latino learners? It means that teachers need to be sensitive to supporting the development of identity as well as language and academics by avoiding potentially threatening practices and providing low-risk/high-impact learning experiences and interactions. Low-risk/high-impact activities engage students in thoughtful and high-level thinking processes, while minimizing risk of embarrassment and anxiety.

One example of low-risk/high-impact engagement is the Biopoem, a poem that describes a person in eleven lines (Abromitis, 1994). Poetry writing can be a self-affirming form of expression that isn't constrained by writing conventions, grammar, or punctuation. Writing poetry can be a daunting task caused by the vulnerability associated with putting your heart on a page. The Biopoem follows a specific template, which decreases the risks yet still provides ample opportunity for students to compellingly reveal significant aspects of themselves. A standard template is below, but it can be changed or tailored to meet specific needs or interests.

## How to Write a Biopoem

Line 1—First name
Line 2—Three or four adjectives that describe you
Line 3—Important relationship (daughter/son/mother of...)
Line 4—Two or three things, people, or ideas that you love
Line 5—Three feelings you've experienced
Line 6—Three fears you've experienced
Line 7—Accomplishments or aspirations (who composed, discovered, etc.)
Line 8—Two or three things you want to see happen or experience
Line 9—Your residence
Line 10—Last name

A sample Biopoem follows on the next page.

<u>**Tammy**</u>

**Compassionate, Strong, Organized, and Thoughtful**

**Mother of Sierra and Alex,**

**Lover of my husband, nature, and reading**

**Who feels thankful, reflective, and fulfilled.**

**Who fears nothing when following God.**

**Who has successfully measured and installed bedroom blinds!**

**Who would like her novel to be turned into a movie.**

**Resident of Chicago,**

**Oberg De La Garza**

## IDENTITY-FRIENDLY PRACTICES

There are many other classroom practices that could potentially cause students extreme discomfort. One commonly misused teaching practice is to randomly call on unprepared students to answer questions or read an unfamiliar text selection. Asking unprepared students to orally present to whole groups is a situation that is rife with danger—the possibility of public failure heavily outweighs any benefit from demonstrating, in front of peers, what is academically expected. Calling on volunteers regularly will overly involve students who are able to quickly formulate answers while speaking and limit students who require a little reflection before speaking.

Perhaps the strongest method of involving all students to actively engage in thinking, formulating ideas, and speaking is Think-Pair-Share. This cooperative discussion strategy can be used in all areas of the curriculum.

- Think – Teachers pose a thoughtful question for the whole class to **think** about and formulate an answer.
- Pair – Students **pair** with a partner to discuss their answers.
- Share – Partners **share** their answers with the whole group.

Not only does this activity reduce risk, but it also establishes a foundation of "we're in it together."

One identity-threatening reading practice is Round Robin—an oral reading style where students read a text section aloud in turn. Teachers use these methods to engage visual, auditory, and even kinesthetic learning styles. The following reading activities are alternatives and potentially less embarrassing to English Language Learners or struggling readers.

Shared Reading: The teacher reads aloud, modeling good fluency and expression while students follow text in their own book. The teacher occasionally pauses to model comprehension strategies. This method provides a safe way for students to explore grade-level (or above) material and new vocabulary.

Buddy/Partner Reading: A weaker reader is paired with a stronger reader, and together they choose a book or text passage. The readers take turns reading or read together. The better reader can help with pronunciation, the meaning of words, and understanding the story. They can ask questions and employ comprehension strategies as they read. This method can be tailored to meet the needs of individual students within a grade, in all content areas, and across grades K–12.

Choral Reading: Small or whole groups read passages aloud in unison. This method is used most effectively in kindergarten through fourth grade and will pull along slower readers and has an attractive musical quality to some students.

Tape/Digital Recorded Reading: This individual or group-reading activity gives students the opportunity to read along in their books as they hear a fluent reader read the book on audiotape. This method builds fluency, pronunciation, the meaning of words, and comprehension of the text. Students can reread/listen to the same passage, take notes, or pause for questions as they read. Taped assisted reading can be flexibly used in all content areas across grades K–12.

## BELONGING IN THE CLASSROOM

Whether Latino students in the mainstream classroom are fluent in English or engaged in learning a second language, the majority are navigating borders that separate distinctly different cultural traditions and practices. Without programs in place to support formal native-language development and culture, Latinos face varying degrees of disconnection between their native culture, familial ties, and rich values and traditions. Beyond superficial "multicultural-awareness weeks," classroom teachers must find ways to support students' connections to native language and heritage.

Expressing genuine interest and curiosity in students' culture, traditions, and experiences is one way to start. By modeling a desire to explore and learn about a new culture, teachers can provide a safe atmosphere for Latino students to do the same. Publicly learning and mispronouncing new words in Spanish enables teachers to experience the challenges associated with taking risks while making it acceptable and inviting for English-Language Learners to make similar advances. *Carmen Learns English* by Judy Cox is a story of a first-grade Spanish speaker who is too frightened to speak in class until she hears her teacher's *muy* (very) ugly Spanish. With a little encouragement from her teacher and classmates, Carmen soon feels safe to practice and quickly master new words in English.

Creating an atmosphere of safety for the whole group and each individual student lays the groundwork for fostering Latino students' positive identity in the classroom. Communicating messages through words and actions that proclaim acceptance for all differences— language, culture, appearance, social status, height, weight, and skin color—meets students' hierarchical need for safety and enables them to move forward to pursue more advanced levels of learning and development.

# CHAPTER 4: TREATMENT AS INDIVIDUALS

*Living on borders and in margins, keeping intact one's shifting and multiple identity and integrity, is like trying to swim in a new element, an "alien" element.*

~Gloria Anzaldua~

Educator, scholar of Chicana cultural theory, social activist, and author of
*Borderlands/LaFrontera: The New Mestiza*

People hold a number of expectations for individuals, and these often manifest in teachers' interactions with their students. Some of these expectations and beliefs can be grounded in experience—a student who does well on the first test is often expected to do well on tests that follow (Aronson & Steele, 2005). Other expectations may be formed out of stereotypes or false beliefs that one holds about an individual and their attributes—these expectations may be connected to social class, race, ethnicity, religion, and gender and may be academic in nature or not.

Stereotypes are images we hold of others that help simplify and organize our worlds and also serve to help us make decisions quickly about what people in certain categories can or cannot do. Although this strategy may help reduce cognitive load and increase information processing, stereotypes are often broad generalizations that oversimplify how we understand human nature. Stereotypes also ignore important individual differences, leaving one open to the threat of making wrong assumptions and constructing false beliefs about others (Aronson & Steele, 2005).

Stereotypes are constructed at an early age partially because they are embedded in society and learned as children begin to organize their worlds (Derman-Sparks, Ramsey, & Edwards, 2003). By elementary school, most students have taken on the beliefs that Blacks and Latinos are less intelligent than White children, Blacks are better athletes than Whites, and girls struggle in math, while Asian students excel (McKown & Weinstein, 2003).

Unfortunately, whether or not students themselves adopt these stereotypes as their own, they are faced with the challenge that others do hold such beliefs. One way this happens is through interactions with peers. Unfortunately, minority children are at the greatest risk of being excluded by peers. This may be a result of social pressures that emerge out of existing stereotypes. For example, Black and Latino students who are academically succeeding can often be targeted as "acting White"—suggesting that Black and Latino students who do well in school are at risk of abandoning their social group (Fordham & Ogbu, 1986). As one can imagine, this is particularly harmful during middle school, a crucial age when academic problems often emerge at a time when fitting in is more important than ever (Aronson & Good, 2002; Wigfield & Eccles, 2002).

Stereotypes in school, whether explicitly addressed or not, haunt students, particularly Black and Latino students and females in male-dominated subject areas (e.g., math and science).

This phenomenon is called stereotype threat and illustrates that feelings of inferiority emerge for students when aspects directly related to stereotypes (e.g., intelligence) are measured and are subsequently related to their test performance. This helps explain, in part, the achievement gap[3] between minority and White students.

---

[3] Similar to the framework of subtractive schooling, scholars have pointed to systematic, normative schooling practices that have marginalized minority student populations and have, subsequently, contributed to said 'achievement gap'. Other structural inequities, such as vast disparities in access to well-resourced and staffed schools, portrays the 'achievement gap' as an 'opportunity gap'.

Although the effect of stereotypes on students paints a grim picture, another important lesson has been learned from this research—the effects of stereotypes and expectations can be modified in ways to support rather than hinder student success. For example, in an experimental study in which women were told that, "This test has never produced gender differences," women's performance increased significantly from the control group in which the participants were told nothing about test performance outcomes (Spencer, Steele, & Quinn, 1999). Furthermore, feedback, regardless of its' accuracy (Baumeister, Twenge, & Nuss, 2002), interventions (Wilson & Linville, 1985), and responses from teachers, such as praise (Mueller & Dweck, 1998), can quickly change a student's outcome from one task to another, and can dramatically alter a student's GPA a year later. Although these findings illustrate that competence is fragile (Aronson & Steele, 2005), they also imply a powerful tool. For example, in one study parents' beliefs predicted their child's self-confidence better than actual performance (Frome & Eccles, 1998). Hence, the expectations that teachers hold and explicit strategies that they use in the classroom to illustrate such expectations can be used to counteract and challenge the negative stereotypes that students face inside and outside of class.

In this next essay, Mayra Carrillo-Daniel introduces stereotypes (both negative and positive) that she, a Cuban immigrant, faces and how she navigates her identity and belonging in both her ethnic group and her current home, the United States. Carrillo-Daniel leads us through everyday mainstream American cultural practices such as dining, music, and talking, in ways that enable those familiar with such customs to recognize potential for misunderstandings caused by cultural differences. Her narrative invites us to consider how making subtle assumptions about members of different cultures can be as hurtful and isolating as blatant expressions of racism.

**WARM-UP BACKGROUND KNOWLEDGE**: Consider what you know about Cuba. Perhaps you have a vague concept of its geographic location or government. What do you know about the people of Cuba? What associations do you carry about their culture?

Cuba is located ninety miles south of Key West, Florida. Originally inhabited by the Arawak Indians, Cuba was invaded and ruled by the Spanish in the early 1500s until the revolution in the 1890s. After the United States won the Spanish American War in 1898, it occupied Cuba and then granted Cuba independence in 1902, after the Platt Agreement gave the United States unlimited power to intervene in Cuba's affairs to protect US interests. After three decades of frequent US political and corporate intervention and a succession of frequently corrupt Cuban leaders, Fidel Castro came into power in 1959. Castro aligned himself with the anti-American sentiments of the Soviet Union, and Cuba became the first communist state in the western hemisphere. In 1961, Cuban exiles trained and armed by the US Central Intelligence Agency (CIA) unsuccessfully attacked Cuba's Bay of Pigs. Despite the US administration's promises of air and naval support, the Cuban exiles were mainly abandoned to die or become imprisoned in Cuba. Supported by Soviet subsidies until economic crashes in the early 1990s, the Socialist reign of terror strengthened its grip on citizens, and they fled from Castro's mantra of "Socialism or Death"—risking death on inner tubes in the ninety-mile stretch of ocean between Cuba and Florida's freedom.

Fidel's reign ended in 2008, and amid health problems at the age of eighty-two, he retired and handed the presidency over to his brother, Raúl. Immigrating Cubans are typically granted political asylum once they reach the United States.

# My Polka-Dotted World

## by Mayra Carrillo-Daniel

### *The United States*

*Cultural clashes are the norm in the lives of immigrants. I am a privileged Latina because my culture group was welcomed by the United States. In fact, the quotas for Cubans entering this nation were lifted in the early 1960s. This means that the US government was sympathetic to the reasons Cubans were seeking asylum. While I have experienced many instances of cultural mismatch since first coming to the United States, I did not always know the whys and was not always able to understand the behaviors of mainstream Anglos until after an event was over or even until many years later. Sometimes I have felt curiosity when seeing behaviors that I do not understand, but the majority of the time, the mismatches put me in the position of the outsider. Many times I questioned if I am the odd one.*

*In this essay I explore my experiences as an eleven-year-old immigrant and now naturalized US citizen. Today, fifty years after arrival, I define myself with a hyphenated identity. I am loyal to Cuba, the country that I knew before its political upheavals as a somewhat democratic nation, and I consider myself lucky to have the rights of citizenship in my adopted land. At the same time, I know that I am no longer just Cuban. I feel that the woman I grew to be is a multicultural, plurilingual soul on whom the gods smiled. Without question I acknowledge the incredible luck that brought my family to North America. However, it would be a lie to not admit that I long to return to my first home, my Cuba. I want to walk the same sidewalks that I covered daily on my way to my elementary school, El Colegio Apostolado. However, I want to return to Cuba to visit but not to stay, because today the United States is home.*

*Neil Diamond's lyrics in the song he dedicated to the New York Puerto Rican parade beautifully highlight my immigrant experience. He did not understand everything he heard the day of the celebration, yet he felt the only way to describe his feelings was to write a song titled "What a Beautiful Noise." In his lyrics he says, "It's a sound that I love, it's the music of life." Acquiring English-language proficiency and understanding everything that went on around me in the United States was not easy. The process involved listening to beautiful noises that slowly became the rhythms of my new world and provided me the vehicle to understand new ways of being.*

**CRITICAL THINKING**: Neil Diamond was inspired by the sounds of a passing Puerto Rican parade wafting up to his New York hotel window, when his daughter, Marjorie, exclaimed, "What a beautiful noise, Daddy!"

What insight does this give into the innocence of a child in terms of appreciating differences in peoples, cultures, and experiences? Do adults seem to have a similar or different capacity?

*As I speak with you through the words of this essay, I share situations that exemplify themes of exile such as moments of pain that turn to joy and become opportunities to reflect and experience personal growth. Because I am both an American citizen and a Cuban American, for the purposes of this conversation, I will use the term American rather than US citizen to describe an individual either born in or who is a naturalized citizen of the US. I am not doing this because I agree with this overused term. This is the way the majority of US citizens define themselves, and my goal is that you understand my words. However, I do believe that an American can be a citizen of North, South, or Central America and that the term is applicable to not only someone born in the United States. I was an American from day one of my life.*

## My cultures: I am…many things
## My Hometown

*My birthplace was a seaport in the northern Cuban province of Las Villas. It was a place very different from where I live now. Our homes did not need central heating, and warmth in the winter was achieved by wearing a sweater. In winter the flowers continued to bloom, and the royal palm trees that so beautifully lined the avenues and parks never lost their leaves. I grew up eating the fruits of the ocean in Caibarién, a city in Cuba known as La Villa Blanca (the white town), known for its sands and beaches. We dined on stone crab, red snapper, and lobster while having no inkling of how some people in other parts of the world dreamt of the delicacies we so frequently consumed. We were called the cangrejeros (crab people). We relished our name. My mouth waters when I think of stone crabs. I fly to Florida when it is the season to purchase cangrejos (crabs), and my family feasts as we grab onto memories that only I hold and my children experience vicariously. Once my family migrated to the United States, it was many years before we could once again sink our teeth into what we then realized had been a privilege of life in the waters ninety miles south of Florida.*

*Going from life in a warm climate where there was no snow to Chicago, Illinois, posed threats and pleasures such as learning to walk on ice and tasting the ice that fell from the sky. Hmmm…the snow was so cold and so wonderfully icy! We adapted yet held tightly to memories old and new. I can go into Google maps and find the church where my parents were married in Remedios. When I do this, I am content to feel my belongingness in two different and now joined worlds. I hear the echoes of my grandmother's words when she and I walked in the church, and she pointed out an altar made of gold.*

### Good-Bye Cuba

*My mother, my brother, and I left Cuba on June 27, 1961, two months after the Bay of Pigs Invasion. This failed effort to free Cuba from communism was a plan initially backed by the US government and the Central Intelligence Agency. However, it was a failure that left the Cubans who disembarked at the mercy of their captors. The United States made promises and then backed off. The biased history books that were used to teach about this encounter in US schools lightly cover an event that changed many lives.*

*What led to Bay of Pigs was the fact that Cuba in 1959 was not a democracy. It was a world of one unstable government after another. Cuba acquired its independence from Spain in 1902, and true democracy had not been achieved by the time Fidel Castro promised equity to all in 1959. Once Castro and his milicianos (militants) came down from the hills in Oriente Province, the promises they made led the masses to hope that change was for the better. Before Castro, Cuba was a nation where illiteracy was rampant, and subsequently the have-nots worked for low wages and could not aspire to what they deserved. Cuba was in the process of evolving into a different country, and many were working to establish a democracy, but the dictatorship that preceded Castro's revolution, coupled with*

*Castro's idealistic communism of nondeliverables destroyed this possibility. This is why so many Cubans went into exile.*

*I am part of the first wave of Cuban immigrants to the United States. We seek to hold on to our Cuban origins in spite of living life almost entirely in the United States. We were a group that left Cuba en masse. Before this time small numbers of Cubans had left their island. It was a moment where thousands of Cubans went into exile in the United States, Mexico, and Spain. We left Cuba thinking Fidel Castro's regime would fall within a couple of years of our departure. We did not leave due to financial reasons, because our life in Cuba was good. We went into exile because we could not live without freedom. When we left, my mother left an oversized chair that she had stuffed with cash in my abuela's house. I also remember the wall in the bedroom that had wooden planks. My uncle moved a couple of these because the chair had not been large enough to accommodate all the cash that we were saving for a rainy day, so we used the wall as our vault. I understand the house is still there and am dying to climb a ladder to see what I find.*

*I am a child/victim of communism who has softened her stance on the 1959 revolution that changed her island. My wish is to be free to return and touch the soil where I was born. I longingly feel that if I could do that, I would be representing the members of the older generations who are no longer with us and the precious few who are still alive. The United States is a land that offered hope to us just as it has done for the many others who have fled their countries.*

*I know that I am no longer just Cuban. I am this mother, wife, and grandmother that my children and family embrace while at times seeking to fully understand. Before grasping what the terms bicultural and bilingual meant, I struggled during my teen years to fit into the new world that my parents had thrust me into. In the United States of the 1960s, I noted that people laughed at what I thought wasn't funny, that they ate what I thought were odd meals such as one-dish casseroles, and that lunch might consist of a peanut-butter and jelly sandwich. However, as time went by, I learned that tuna casserole was tasty and that grape jelly made for a mean sandwich. In the early '70s, I began to laugh at Bob Hope and Archie Bunker as well as get the subtle humor of the Johnny Carson Show. I was still Cuban, but I was developing a bicultural identity. I had traveled from noticing surface features to understanding that cultural differences matter.*

*I am Cuban and a child of many colors. In academic circles the term "child of color" is defined to include a person's complexion and/or ethnic origin. My daughter and I discussed my phenotype one day when she was a student at the University of Illinois at Urbana-Champaign. She thought the term "child of color" encapsulated me. I told her I was a Cuban Caucasian. She told me that together, these adjectives had not been once mentioned in her curriculum. My quick and somewhat flippant comment to her was that I was not polka-dotted. I argued that placing anyone in such a general category was an attempt to offer a quick and simple description. I am certain that my identity was shaped by my experiences of life within two cultural groups, which each held a different language as the medium of schooling and business. Arriving at a single descriptor does not acknowledge the stages of development that I have and will continue to travel through in my life. I know that this statement may be questioned, but it is my belief that who one is consists of more than one set of qualities, be these implicit or explicit, that can be easily ascribed to a definition.*

**CRITICAL THINKING**: What are the stereotypes that you hold about immigrants? Think about the word "immigrant" and write down the first five words that you associate with this term.

*Some might ask what exactly I consider myself to be, since it would be easier to accept that I am a child of color. The terms that I use to define my culture and my identity are crystal clear to me. Therein lies a conflict that is unspoken and unnoticed by some who surround me. I fit into crowds with my light skin and green eyes, yet I am neither this nor that. I am the juncture of the two cultures that have had the greater influence on me, the American and the Cuban cultures, plus the added bits and pieces of what I have admired in people I have met in my travels. It always amazes me that I am assumed to be a native-born Illinoisan until I share a bit of my story. Then I am told that I have an accent when I speak English. How I can develop an accent from one minute to the next? The reality must be that when mainstream Americans hear a person is an immigrant, they think an accent is a piece of the pie. This happens with people who I know intend to offer a compliment, and so I take it this way.*

*I believe that I am this great mix of the best and the worst of my two cultures. Every day that passes, something reminds me that my identity is influenced by the visible and invisible pieces of the Cuban and American identities that live in me. Some of these characteristics are admirable while others suggest the many ways that discriminatory attitudes and arrogance are present in all of us regardless of our ethnicity, religion, socioeconomic status, educational achievements, and immigrant experience. Ethnocentrism, the belief that one's culture is better than all others, is an undesirable quality and a hard one to eliminate.*

*My Cuban roots propelled me to develop my identity beginning at the ethnocentric stages of my family members. I was told that Cubans were different from other immigrant groups. We were better. We could justify our reasons for leaving our country. It was not that we had been poor and uneducated. The reasons shared with me in adolescence made sense to someone who had lived in a protected cocoon. For a time I believed Cuban Spanish to be of a higher quality than other dialects of Spanish. I accepted as facts what I later acknowledged to be untruths as the boundaries of my personal frontiers expanded. Numerous other misconceptions that were part and parcel of my family life I now recognize and label as blatant, ethnocentric, discriminatory behaviors. I do not know if ethnocentrism for immigrant groups weaves their path to survival, but I know the arrogance that rides next to it prevents adaptation and appreciation of "the other" (Bhaba 1994).*

## The Start of Life in the United States: Visitation Grade School near Garfield Boulevard

*Transporting myself back to 1961, I see that I am a lucky immigrant because my mother speaks English. She and the school principal discuss the reasons we left Cuba before my life in a seventh-grade classroom begins. My mother makes sure that I am not placed back a grade or two because I only speak Spanish. On day one of the school year, I am given a multiple-choice test to complete. I stare at it and wonder how I can attack the task, since I do not understand a single word on the page. Thankfully, a few minutes later, I am rescued. The same person who gave me the exam scurries over and takes it away. The nun must have figured out that she was giving me an exam written in a language that I did not understand. I guess even then, my phenotype confused those who could not see past surface features. I must not have looked like an immigrant even in my used uniform and well-ironed blouse from the Salvation Army.*

**CLASSROOM CONNECTION**: In this classroom encounter, the nun/teacher initially makes an assumption about Mayra's ability to take a written exam in English. She then removes the exam after recognizing Mayra has not been able to write a single word. What assumptions did the teacher make about Mayra *prior* to giving her the exam? On what basis did the teacher base her assumptions?

What assumptions do you think the teacher might have after taking away the blank exam?

*I had chicken pox that year. I do not remember learning anything the entire year. There was no help for immigrant non-English speakers in this Chicago school in 1961. However, in every classroom there is a wall filled with books. I read them as best I can. I use what I know to try to understand the books available to me. I am lucky because I am a good reader, and I have a solid educational base. I am smart, and I know it. I skipped third grade in Cuba, and I know that I can learn anything. I am my own English-as-a-second-language teacher. I persevere. I read every book in the class library. I read a book series called Five Little Peppers. Perhaps it was titled differently, but this is what I remember.*

*Every day at Visitation Grade School, I wait for lunch. I am certain that my family's lack of financial resources was a part of the conversation that my mother had with the school principal when she enrolled me in school. From day one I am asked to keep the lunch lines straight and am rewarded with a free lunch. I don't think I do anything, but I have access to a free lunch the entire year, and no one bothers me as I walk up and down the area where the students line up by the cafeteria. Lunchtime is good, too, because I have two cousins who come to the United States midyear, Hebe and Dinah, who move next door and sit with me at lunch. We share my meal.*

*Spaghetti was not commonplace in Cuba, so we don't need too much to be satisfied. We share my spaghetti. Dinah and I are the same age, and Hebe is three years older, but somehow Hebe and I are placed in the same grade and Dinah one year behind. Were our academic levels evaluated in any way? To this day I assume that my mother may not have been present to fight for my cousins when they registered for school as she was for me.*

CRITICAL THINKING: How does prior educational experience in a student's home country shape their experiences in the United States? What questions do teachers need to ask about a student's prior educational experience?

## *Money and Racial Issues*

*Money was an issue because we didn't have much when we arrived in the United States. In Cuba we went to the country club and swam on our private beach where only blancos (Caucasians) were allowed. Once in Chicago, my mother was afraid to walk to the grocery store where things were cheaper because it was a poorer African American area. The store was about ten blocks away. She did not feel comfortable going there, but she had no choice. Chicken could be bought there for only ten cents a pound, so the family would make the weekly adventurous trek. We would walk close together and be admonished to be careful even when the adults were walking alongside of us. The color of the skin of those who lived in our Sangamon Street neighborhood made where we lived appear safer than the area of the grocery store. In Cuba we had lived in a Caucasian world, and a 100 percent African American neighborhood was in stark contrast to our previous life. Discrimination based on race was different in Cuba. Cubans of different phenotypes would socialize, but they set boundaries that were different from those in the United States of the 1960s. My parents understood their own discriminatory practices, but those they observed in this country were unfamiliar and incomprehensible to them.*

*My parents would comment that neighborhoods were segregated in the United States and that Blacks could not use the same bathrooms or eat in the same restaurants as Caucasians. Perhaps their observations contributed to my mother's fear of African Americans in the United States. The racial climate within this country was incomprehensible to her, so she withdrew in fear. Even some twenty years later, my mom's ethnocentrism was such a part of her that she was still afraid to take a taxi driven by a black man. I remember a trip to the Art Institute of Chicago and her refusal to get into the first cab that came to pick us up because the driver was an African American. I wonder if she simply never felt safe in the United States or if she ever adapted to life in this country?*

**BACKGROUND KNOWLEDGE**: Immigrants from every country and culture face discrimination and stereotyping to varying extents— particularly during the 1960s racial tensions and Civil Rights Movement. In the early 1960s, certain populations were complaining that 1920s immigration quotas discriminated against them in favor of Western Europeans.

The Immigration and Nationality Act of 1965 changed the 1920s quotas of immigrants who were able to enter the United States. It established a preference system that prioritized immigrants based on skills and family relationships with US citizens or residents. US demographics changed profoundly with immigrants from Asia, Africa, the Middle East, as well as Latin America.

### Collecting Bottles for Pennies

*In 1961 soda pop came in bottles, and the price included a deposit of two cents per bottle. When I saw bottles on the street, I would pick them up. Either Chicago was a little safer then, or my family did not understand the dangers of a young teen walking up and down the street picking up bottles. Five bottles equaled ten cents. At the five-and-dime, my earnings bought me a small bag of peanuts or candy. Transistor radios cost but a few dollars. I saved my money and bought my first piece of electronics. I purchased my radio at the same store where we bought the cheap chicken. Chicago was good to me. My parents were proud that I was resourceful.*

### Adolescence to Adulthood in the United States
### Fifty Years Later: You Are Different

*In my workplace there are people employed from many parts of the world. A couple of years ago, a colleague said to me, "Well, you know you are different, don't you?" I am not sure what she meant. Is it my Cuban identity still? I must allow my friend to label me as she wishes because I simply do not know how else to be. I am simply the reflection of the years of my life, and so is she.*

*In this next section, I touch upon events that involved me in examining mainstream practices in this country when I least expected it. My focus on holidays is in no way superficial. Underlying components of what makes us different are visible in the way we gather and celebrate moments of time. I am sharing situations and reflecting upon experiences that helped me understand both US culture and myself more deeply.*

## Celebrations and Assumptions the American Way: Holidays and Customs

*The joys of Halloween unfolded one wonderful day in Chicago when I discovered that one could go house-to-house and get candy. Imagine free Milky Ways! My cousins and I went out together that first year. The only problem was that I was five feet one and a little too big to trick-or-treat. When one of my classmates opened her front door and commented that we were too big, I realized there would be no more free candy. Cuban holidays do not include Halloween, and from that day on, I have loved the day. I also embraced other holidays celebrated in the United States as my own because the new traditions that I observed in others were fun.*

*Visits from the Easter Bunny evolved as I had children. Easter Sunday came to include Mass plus a hunt for Easter eggs. At about age twenty-nine, I learned from my husband how children in Iowa hunt for eggs on Easter Sunday. My brother and I never had an egg hunt, and it seemed an interesting and easy event to plan. This did not mean that I denied the religious traditions that my family had held but that I added new customs to the repertoire.*

*On a beautiful spring day in college, I discovered the tradition of May Day flowers and baskets. The first time I received a May basket, I loved the idea, so I quickly made one for George, my boyfriend. I prepared his gift, wrote on it "Happy May Day Thursday," and left it on his doorstep. He explained the holiday took place on May first, and the day was not always the first Thursday of May. This was the same day that his mother visited him in college. The May Day tradition then became intertwined with issues of race and prejudice. George told me that when his mother discovered he was dating a Cuban, she inquired about the color of my skin. When I later met her, I saw that my skin was lighter than her Lebanese olive complexion. To this day when I reveal that I am Cuban, the conversation always touches on my phenotype. I have very pale skin, and somehow many people in the United States assume that Cubans are dark. I have learned to calmly explain that in my family we might have green or blue eyes and light skin and that yes, I am 100 percent Cuban. I am often asked if my father was stationed at Guantanamo Bay.*

**CLASSROOM CONNECTION**: Students may ask similar questions to an immigrant student. As a teacher, how do you respond to these comments and questions?

*The May Day experience highlighted for me that the misconceptions that some have about immigrants are due to a lack of knowledge, while others reflect their personal experiences. I chose to ignore my future mother-in-law's comment and focused on May Day only. I soon found out that my boyfriend's mother was a first-generation Lebanese who as a child growing up in Iowa had not been allowed to spend time in the sun. She tanned well, and her mother never wanted her to stand out. I grasped her unresolved fear that her family would be rejected in mainstream society due to the color of their skin. My future in-laws came to accept me, but I did always wonder if they did so more quickly because I was pretty, my father was the doctor who drove a Cadillac, and my parents at first glance looked and acted like mainstream folks.*

### What Is a Thank-You Note?

*Writing notes of thanks is less common today than it was in the 1960s, but the custom continues to be taught to many children as they grow up in the United States. It is lovely to express appreciation when someone is thoughtful. I love this American custom! Cubans do not write thank-you notes in the methodical polite ways that Americans do. I never wrote a thank-you note until I was graduating high school because the custom of demonstrating appreciation this way was not familiar to me until then. Cubans express their thanks in other ways. It is great to be able to choose to adopt customs from another culture. This is one of the benefits of living in different countries. When I discovered this particular custom, I concluded that writing an official thank-you is a great way to express one's appreciation to another person! I shudder when I think back to the many times that my mother should have sent her thanks and did not before she became aware of the custom. This is a classic example of the errors that one makes when unaware of the cultural norms of a society. It takes much time to adapt to a different world, and it sure can be an eye-opening experience!*

## Dinner in an Anglo Home

*It was a few years after coming to the United States before I was invited to an Anglo classmate's home for dinner. By then I was in my first year of high school. This first meal wasn't a celebration of any sort, but the evening was a learning experience. The family sat at the table just as we did at home. They ate on a tablecloth and had nice dishes. This was where the similarities ended. My fourteen-year-old eyes must have been as big as saucers as the meal unfolded. It was a great meal but nothing like what I was used to. Before dinner they prayed. Then when the meal came, it was a one-dish dinner. I was served something called goulash. I expected other dishes to be served before dessert, but goulash was it. Many years later the first time I visited my fiancé's home in Iowa, I was surprised that they always prayed before dinner, too.*

*Why pray before dinner, I wondered? I had never experienced this in Cuba. I did not know if this was a tradition held and practiced by every family in the United States or only by select families. Now I realize that it is not possible to make a generalization about what people do in the United States. I noted differences and lacked the maturity to appreciate what seemed unfamiliar. I now understand the before-meal prayer may be more of a standard practice in religious homes, and I hypothesize that it is more likely to occur within families that sit down to share meals. If this is true, then issues of socioeconomic status may contribute to the tradition. Although many families eat on the run for many good reasons, back in the 1960s, life was a bit less hectic than it is in the year 2012. Did more real families back then resemble television's Ozzie and Harriet?*

*My reaction to the short prayer before dinner now seems in itself to be what is surprising. My family practiced Catholicism, and I was used to attending long masses conducted in Latin in Cuba. Clearly, my church's ceremonies were part of the person who emigrated to the United States, and I was comfortable with these components of my daily life. My US experience did not reflect my life as I knew it in Cuba. I was experiencing and reacting to my new world but not examining the changes that were being offered to the immigrant child. As a youngster I considered it normal to pray every night before going to sleep. The prayer that I would recite with my mother was music to my ears as well as an integral part of my existence. I did not want to pray before dinner because it was not my family's tradition. Now I share my mother's prayer with my grandson before I kiss him good night. We say, "Angel de la guardia, dulce compañía, no me dejes solo ni de noche ni de día. Cuatro pilares tiene mi cama, cuatro angelitos que me la guardan. Acuestate Aidan y duerme bien" (Guardian angel, dear companion, do not leave me alone night or day. Four pillars has my bed, four angels that guard me. Lie down Aidan and sleep well). After the prayer we also said the words that constituted my good-night Cuban tradition. We say, "Que sueñes con los angelitos y que duermas bien" (May you sleep with the angels and may you sleep well). The prayer and the evening good-bye take me back to Cuba, to where I felt safe and loved. It is not that I do not feel OK where I am now, but my heart has two homes. I respect my husband's right to say a prayer before holiday meals, and he accepts that a daily prayer before supper is not a daily event in our home.*

### Thanksgiving: What do Cubans Have to Do with Pilgrims?

*It was a bit of a family joke that we celebrated Thanksgiving Day with the family together for a meal. I remember my mother joking that we had no ties to the Pilgrims. Today this seems ridiculous considering that we were a more recent version of the group who left England to escape political and religious persecution. I know that my arrogance came through when I would comment to friends about how this very American holiday meant nothing to me. For a long time, I would explain that the day was not part of my childhood. My uncle Lorenzo always said that turkey has no taste. Were we resisting adaptation to the United States? Even today I perceive the holiday as a day off work and a perfect day for my children to visit and nothing more. I do not view the holiday as one to which I attach sentimental value. If given the choice, I would prefer to travel to Mexico, eat the fresh fish they call huachinango (snapper), and skip the turkey. Please notice that trips to Mexico are an ongoing theme in my life. Due to the political issues involving travel for native-born Cubans, I have chosen Mexico as my third homeland. Of course, I do not really fit in the landscape there. I look like a güera (too light-skinned), and I travel with an English-speaking mate. For me the best turkeys are those that I prepare with mojo cubano (Cuban marinade) made following my grandmother's recipe wherever I may be.*

*Somehow along the way as my family adapted to our new existence as citizens of the United States, we began to say grace at Thanksgiving and Christmas. We had been influenced by the American experience. This lovely custom became ours! Of course, we have always celebrated Nochebuena (Christmas Eve) on December 24 because this is what Cubans do. To this day it is the family gathering for dinner on the twenty-fourth that matters to me. The twenty-fifth is for other purposes. The cultures within me take turns surfacing and overpowering each other.*

**BACKGROUND KNOWLEDGE**: Nochebuena is a custom in Spain, Latin American, and the Philippines that is held on the evening before Christmas and consists of a traditional dinner with family.

\* The Cuban and Puerto Rican tradition is a family dinner centered around a pig roast, or *lechón*, with many side dishes and desserts.

\* In Spain, dinner with family and friends is held after Christmas Mass. It is particularly common to start the meal with a seafood dish followed by a bowl of hot, homemade soup. It is also common to have desserts.

\* In some countries of Latin America, dinner served with the family after Mass is known as *Misa de Gallo* and marks the final evening of the *Posadas* celebrations.

\* In New Mexico, la Nochebuena is celebrated by lighting *luminarias* (small bonfires) and *farolitos* (paper lanterns—commonly a candle set in some sand inside a paper bag).

## Keeping my Cubanness: College, Marriage, and Becoming a Grandmother

*Not necessarily intending to do so, my family helped me to value my heritage in many subtle ways. Immigrants do this because their culture is within them, and their actions evidence who they are. There were few Cubans where we lived in our rural Illinois area when I was a teenager, but they were all my parents' friends. I liked it when they visited. As a teen I learned how to welcome afternoon visitors. The greeting is always accompanied with a kiss on the cheek whether one is an adult or a child. One makes café cubano (Cuban coffee) and serves it in tiny little cups.*

*Like all good Cubans, we vacationed in Miami Beach in the summer. I make this generalization because when we traveled to Miami, my parents held court at the hotel every evening. Friends and family who lived there as well as those vacationing would get together and fill the hotel lobby. Thanks to these trips, I was privy to the cultural nuances that I might have lost growing up in a community where the only Cubans were my family members. I learned that in conversations Cubans interrupt each other and do not take turns as Americans do.*

**CRITICAL THINKING**: How do you think the author became aware of this? Do you suspect she changed her behavior around certain individuals because of this awareness?
How might this custom be perceived by others who do not practice it?

*Even today I continue to make efforts during conversations with Anglos to not interrupt the person who is speaking. I work hard to control my enthusiasm. However, I do not want to take the Cuban out of me, and I grasp fiercely to keep what is still untouched by my American identity. The trips to Florida that seemed boring to a teenager now compose my more precious memories.*

### The University of Iowa

*My going off to college required my mother to behave in a non-Cuban way. Thanks to Mom I became an Iowa Hawkeye. She uncharacteristically stood up to the dominating force in the family, my father. He wanted me to attend a private college, live with relatives in Chicago, and not go off to a large, state-funded college alone. My mother's behavior defending me was unusual for her, and never again did I see this strength surface. After we came to the United States, she behaved like the more traditional Cuban wife. Perhaps it was because my father achieved the same status level in the United States that he had in Cuba, and she did not. In the United States, she was never able to practice her profession.*

*Starting college at the University of Iowa brought many surprises. I had never been to a football game and had hardly dated. I was the first to attend a university in the United States in my family. When I asked if I could join a sorority, my father replied that no, I could not live in an old house when there were new dormitories available. While at Iowa I realized that if I did not call home when the weekend started, I would receive a late-evening call from the family to make sure I was not out late. Although I was permitted to live in my college town, I was expected to be in by 10:00 p.m. As a bicultural being, I found a solution. I called home every Friday evening about 7:30 to tell the family about my week. I knew they would not show distrust and check up on me. I was free to be an American, bilingual, bicultural college student. I also met the requirements of being a Cuban daughter.*

*At Iowa I had to decide if I wanted to date Anglos or Latinos. Why date a Latino? I thought Latinos are, well, are not what I want. They are bossy. I decided I wanted a man with a great sense of humor. I dated Anglos. I liked tall, dark-haired Anglos who looked Cuban. I married one. He is of Lebanese descent, and he is bossy. I married the same guy whose mother feared before meeting me that my skin color would be dark. The Iowan I married fits the Cuban stereotype in some ways. Although I wanted to date mainstream Anglos, I found a man whose family values and traditions were aligned to mine.*

### Music in My Home

*I love Cuban music. There is nothing like a good song. At college I listened to Celia Cruz at the same time that I would play Credence Clearwater Revival and Bob Dylan. I also enjoy rhythms from other parts of Latin America. With the music of Juan Luis Guerra from the Dominican Republic, I can dream my days away and work very effectively. My husband did not like my Spanish music for many years. He would ask me to turn it off. This was a problem. I kept playing my music. I am not sure when he became bicultural in his tastes, but we now live listening to songs whose lyrics he does not understand.*

### Aidan's Abi

*I have a grandson, Aidan, whose name does not translate well to Spanish. When I chose my children's names, my husband and I found choices that would work in both of our cultures and languages. My daughter did not have this concern. Since my arrival in the United States, I have had two names: one is my name in*

81

*Spanish, the other my name pronounced American-style. I do not like my American name.*

*Names matter. The decision of what my grandson would call me took some time for my family. My daughter married a first-generation Mexican American who seems to perceive himself to be more American than Mexican. It's interesting that when he washes his car, the music he listens to is in Spanish. I believe he is more bicultural than he realizes. In his family's culture, one does not call a grandmother abuela but abuelita. The latter is an endearing term. I argued that I am not Mexican but Cuban and that to call me abuela would not be disrespectful. Since I loved the old television show Bewitched, I proposed "Grandmama" as a suitable option, but that was vetoed by my daughter for not being Cuban enough. My husband decided he had the right word, and since his Spanish is limited, he chose to call me habichuela (green bean). I answered to habichuela for a few months, and when I dressed in green, it always evoked a chuckle. In the end the troops chose a very sweet name for me. I am Abi, pronounced as a Spanish word, which in English sounds like AhBee and reflects the beginning of habichuela.*

*I have not shared the name that my children called my father and that the family came to call him. As in all cultures, names change when you have a beautiful toddler playing with language. Yes, we have much in common across our cultures and generational roles regardless of our culture group. My very serious father was named Martin, but his first grandchild baptized him anew. He became Tin Tin to his four grandchildren. I should have put this in parentheses on his gravestone: "Here lies Tin Tin, loved abuelo to Ani, Marty, Alex, and Will."*

### Today: My Political Stance

*My observations lead me to conclude that many in the United States would like to create a definition for who a citizen of this nation should be. In addition, public opinion echoes what needs to be done here and abroad and offers reasons why the United States must expand its democratic borders and colonize those who have other ways of being. These individuals may hold political office or may be the lady who serves lunch in a highly Mexican Pilsen grade school in the city of Chicago. Those who feel that the borders of this nation should be closed have ethnocentric attitudes. They have not analyzed the immigrant experience.*

*I choose to adapt rather than assimilate so that it is possible to communicate with not only people who speak and think in English. This widens my world. Some believe that immigrants should learn English and that it does not matter if they pass their mother tongue to their children. These are the folks whom we need to help understand that growing up bilingual is the gift of an all-terrain vehicle that provides cognitive advantages to learners (Garcia, 2009). The benefits of biculturalism also escape those who have not had the privilege of becoming a citizen of two nations. I hope this essay serves to open eyes to the possibilities of living lives that embrace and applaud walking to the beat of beautiful noises.*

*My bicultural past and present have informed, guided, and enriched my personal and professional lives. In my work I teach teachers who have returned to college to prepare to work with learners from other countries. In each course that I teach, I share a personal story of struggle and triumph. I did not use to do this but have found that it breaks barriers and helps us laugh and learn. Next year I look forward to working with undergraduate future teachers and helping them to be ready for all learners in our schools. I object to the current trends in education espoused by people who do not know how long it takes to adapt to a new culture and to learn a new language. I am on a mission, and it is an important one. Had I been taught under No Child Left Behind and tested to death, I may never have attended college or maintained pride in being Cuban. I feel a deep responsibility to take care of children and families who do not speak English as a first language. I also believe that all children born in the United States have the right to be more than monolingual. I had parents who could fight for me. My mother told the nuns at Visitation Grade School when she registered me that I had finished sixth grade in Cuba and so would enroll in seventh. She was my personal champion.*

*My one sibling does not appear to have the same ties to the family's first culture that I have. He came to this country at age five, and he now seems more like an Iowan than anything else. I believe it is the female who more tenaciously holds on to family traditions. I see my daughter rear her child with the wish and the will that he be bilingual and multicultural. I wonder whom my son will marry and if he will have bilingual or multilingual children. I hope so.*

*My husband and I created a home for our children that included dogs who came and fetched when spoken to in English and Spanish. Our children studied abroad during their undergraduate years and are aware of the many privileges their diversity provided them. Our friends learned to savor and asked for the recipe to puerco asado (roast pork Cuban-style). My daughter teaches in a Chicago public school in Pilsen, a predominantly Mexican American neighborhood, where her students notice the Cuban accent in her Spanish and love her. My son, to the family's surprise, loves to date ladies from China. We feel lucky to have boundaries in our lives that are fluid.*

*A few days ago, a cable-television repairman came to my house. I did not open the door for him nor did I speak to him. The man told my husband that his wife is from Costa Rica. My husband reports that one of the first things the man did was ask if I was Cuban. The second comment from the repairman was that our house looked like a Cuban's home. I took this as a compliment and so did my husband.*

**About the author:** Mayra Carrillo-Daniel, a native of the island of Cuba, emigrated to the United States with her family at age ten to escape communism. In her work with K–12 teachers, she shares the philosophy that the schoolhouse must applaud and promote all children's rights to their plurilingual and pluricultural identities.

# Take It to the Classroom:

## Beyond Cultural Responsiveness

In her essay, Mayra Carrillo-Daniel offered insight into cultural differences and missteps—instances of false interpretations and missed assumptions. Americans are typically socialized to conform to society's bias toward race, class, gender, and sexual orientation. Blatant, "old-fashioned" racism no longer poses the biggest threat to people of color; rather, it is the modern form of racism known as racial microaggressions that create hostile climates for diverse peoples (Solórzano, Ceja, & Yosso, 2000). Due to the subverted visibility of microaggressions, Whites typically do not recognize microaggressions as anything more than minor misunderstandings and quickly dismiss such encounters. Research, however, demonstrates that the negative impact of microaggressions is associated with creating negative racial climate and feelings of self-doubt, isolation, and frustration (Sue, 2010), attacking the emotional and mental well-being of recipients (Sue, Capodilupo, & Holder, 2008), and devaluing of social-group identities (Purdie-Vaughns et al., 2008).

The instances of microaggression that took place in Mayra's vignettes varied in degree of perceptibility and communicated derogatory racial slights or dismissive, sweeping assumptions (Steele, Spencer, & Aronson, 2002). With microaggressions come unspoken messages. The following table organizes several examples from Mayra's essay by theme, microaggression, and message.

| Theme | Microaggression | Message |
|---|---|---|
| Criminal Status Assumption: a person of color is assumed to be dangerous/a criminal. | *"my mother was afraid to walk to the grocery store where things were cheaper because it was a poorer African American area."* | People of color are criminals and/or dangerous. People of color are poor and going to steal. |
| Second-class citizen: preferential treatment given to White people over people of color. | *"To this day when I reveal that I am Cuban the conversation always touches on my phenotype. I have very pale skin and somehow many people in the United States assume that Cubans are dark."* | Whites are more valued than people of color. |
| Alien in own land: Latino Americans are assumed to be foreign born. | *"well, you know you are different, don't you?"* *"I am often asked if my father was stationed at Guantanamo Bay."* | You are not a true American. You are a foreigner. |

**Figure 4.1** *Microaggressions and messages*

Misunderstandings between cultures are catalysts for microaggressions. Mayra's essay provides numerous opportunities to explore the unfamiliar dance steps between Cubans and Whites—from the seemingly insignificant matter of writing thank-you notes to the larger-than-life problems of identity and language. Peeling back the layers of cultural nuances helps us understand and accept each other's differences—across all races.

## BATTLING RACISM IN THE CLASSROOM

Current-day classrooms are filled with Latino students where cultural misunderstandings and stereotypes are propagated—among school personnel, faculty, and even students themselves. Recognizing that racism and ethnocentrism are learned attributes, it would seem that an educational setting would be the ideal place to begin the eradication of hateful thinking.

It has already been noted that only 18 percent of teachers represent the cultural diversity of students in public schools across the nation (USDE, 2016). Research demonstrates that teachers who do not share the cultures of their students *can* provide culturally sustaining instruction if they understand their students' ways of knowing, doing, and existing within their home culture (Halcón, 2001; Moll 2001; Ogbu, 2001). Becoming this culturally responsive teacher is a necessary first step before creating a classroom culture where all students are accepted, supported, and afforded the best opportunity to learn.

Cultural, racial, and societal biases permeate the value system of every individual, including ours. No individual is eager to confront the notion that their values might reflect prejudice toward certain groups; however, it is critical for us to examine our personal histories, thoughts, and experiences to root out preconceptions. Otherwise, there is a very real threat that our blindness will damage relationships with students and parents who represent groups outside our own.

## CULTURALLY SUSTAINING TEACHERS

With knowledge comes a greater understanding of self and others and a greater appreciation of differences (Richards, Brown, & Forde, 2006). Developing cultural competence provides teachers with a foundation for engaging in culturally sustaining pedagogy[4] (Paris,

---

[4] Paris (2012) offers the term culturally sustaining pedagogy to acknowledge the "value of our multiethnic and multilingual present and future. Culturally sustaining pedagogy seeks to perpetuate and foster—to sustain—linguistic, literate, and cultural pluralism as part of the democratic project of schooling." (p. 93)

2012), practices that have been previously identified as culturally responsive or relevant (Cazden & Leggett, 1976; Gay 2002; Ladson-Billings, 1995; Villegas & Lucas, 2002).

1) *Reflective Thinking & Writing*—Teachers must reflectively evaluate their motivations, actions, and/or interactions to discern how their behaviors are governed. Developing a sociocultural consciousness means recognizing that our thoughts, actions, and existence are shaped by race, social class, ethnicity, and language. Asking, "Why did I say/do/think that specific thing that nags at my consciousness?" is a good start to a reflective journal entry. Understanding the factors that contribute to ethnocentrism/racism is the first step toward change.

2) *Explore Personal and Family History*—Having knowledge of the roots and early experiences of one's life will help a teacher identify where/when a specific thought pattern began. Speaking informally with family members about their beliefs of their own race compared to the race or ethnicity of other groups will reveal the historical shaping of personal values. Asking the question, "What was the biggest question I had to deal with, growing up?" will yield telling insights.

3) *Acknowledge Membership in Different Groups*—Teachers need to recognize their membership in different groups of society and identify the advantages and disadvantages that are associated with each. For example, a white, female teacher who belongs to the middle class has certain powers and privileges afforded to her because of social class but has obstacles because of her gender in a male-oriented world.

4) *Awaken to History and Experience of Other Groups*—The first step toward increased cultural competence is to rethink our assumptions and consider life's problems from the perspective of people who have different cultural backgrounds than ours (Sleeter, 1995). Teachers of Latino students need to research the history of the Latino people in the United States in order to understand the rich history of geography, religion, and language changes imposed on a people who are being forced to assimilate to the colonized nation. For example, *Latino Americans* is a six-hour PBS documentary covering five hundred years of history and featuring interviews with nearly one hundred Latinos (http://www.pbs.org/latino-americans/en/). This informative film is helpful in understanding how different historical experiences have shaped the Latino perspective.

5) *Develop an Appreciation of Diversity*—"To be effective in a diverse classroom, teachers must have an appreciation of diversity" (Richards, Brown, & Forde, 2006, p. 7). Teachers' attitudes, interactions, relationships, and classrooms should broadcast being different or unique is the "norm," while rejecting the impression that any single group or value system is more capable than another.

Teachers must cultivate their personal attributes that enable them to champion the unique qualities of each individual, without taking into consideration gender, race, culture, language, social status, or value system. Without this characteristic, a teacher cannot effectively provide a just, educational experience for all students.

## LEVELS OF CULTURALLY SUSTAINING INSTRUCTION

Equally important to academic advancement is the teacher's responsibility to provide opportunities for students to expand their awareness of cultural diversity and learn acceptance of others (Putnam,

1998). Differing levels of culturally sustaining instruction can be woven into every aspect of classroom life, and it is the teacher's responsibility to make intentional and deliberate decisions about the level and type of diversity in the curriculum that will set the tone for critical reflection, self-analysis, and change.

Pulling from the work of culturally responsive instruction, we explore three levels of instruction that seeks to sustain students' cultures: exclusive, inclusive, and transformed (Morey & Kilano, 1997). The exclusive level is bounded by a specific span of time and typically touches the surface four Fs of diverse cultures: food, fun, folklore, and fashion. The content of this level of diversity exploration is stuck at mainstream experiences that contribute to, rather than deconstruct, stereotypes. Instruction at this level is teacher-centered and typified with lecture, reading, and multiple-choice exams.

The inclusive level of diversity instruction remains teacher centered but widens the scope and adds some dimension by adding diversity but keeps it in contrast to the dominant norm. Content delivery may include use of guest speakers and texts authored by individuals with varying perspectives or social views. Instruction encourages students to employ critical thinking and peer learning to construct their own value systems.

Transformed levels of culturally sustaining instruction challenges traditional views and encourages a change in thinking and seeing the world. It is no longer constrained by time (e.g., Hispanic Heritage Month); rather, it shows up in formal and informal activities across the academic time and space. Instruction is student-centered, featuring service learning, problem solving, and/or student-created projects to address needs and answer intrinsic questions. Students learn from each other and the exploration of personal experiences. This may involve exposure to vignettes of real-life situations where an examination of values can be employed. Self-reflection and assessment are characteristic of this level of instruction.

# DIFFERENTIATED INSTRUCTION WITH STUDENTS

For three decades, there has been a disproportionate representation of Latino students in high-incidence special-education classrooms, which is concerning (Klingner et al., 2005). Research demonstrates that one of the leading factors to this disparity is teachers' lack of knowledge about culturally and linguistically diverse students. This unfamiliarity with cultural diversity incorrectly labels students into behavioral categories of unmotivated, negative, and inappropriate (Klinger et al., 2005; Villegas & Lucas, 2002). Once teachers embrace the belief that culturally and linguistically diverse students can be successful and benefitted by their native cultures, languages, and heritage, classroom instruction will genuinely reflect those values and provide equitable learning opportunities for all students.

Providing a quality education that is individually relevant involves the adaption of teaching and learning activities to meet the diverse needs of students. Differentiated instruction addresses students' wide spectrum of academic abilities, prior knowledge, experiences, readiness, language, culture, learning preferences, and interests. In order to reach each student, a teacher must develop distinct and unique paths for students to follow to achieve instructional goals (MCUE, 2008). There is not a single pathway for differentiating instruction within a diverse classroom; however, teachers follow basic principles to guide the journey.

- Assessment is closely aligned to instruction. Teachers use information from formal and informal measures to plan instruction.
- Respectful attitudes toward all students' experiences and cultures are reflected in the worth placed on all students' learning activities, work, and products.
- Flexible grouping enables students to work with a wide variety of student differences. Students may work within a

similar ability-level group, mixed ability-level group, interest-based, or randomly assigned group.

- Best-practice instruction is established that includes cooperative learning, learning centers, technology, and balanced literacy.
- Assessment should include a wide variety of formal and informal methods: portfolios, observations, work samples, writing responses, oral performances, drawings, student work, quizzes/tests, and standardized tests.

Following culturally responsive, differentiated instructional strategies requires practice and time to develop. Revisiting and testing the unconscious thoughts and messages about people, ideas, and practices that are different from our own is a critical practice in battling racism. Incorporating culturally responsive personal and professional-growth activities can be the difference for Latinos and Latinas in your classroom and world.

# CHAPTER 5: ACCESSING CULTURE THROUGH LANGUAGE

*Language is the laughter of the soul.*

~Pablo Neruda~

Chilean poet-diplomat

What is culture? Throughout this text and in this essay in particular, essayists explore culture, often a foggy combination of social practices, language, customs, values, and religion, to name just a few examples. According to Cole (2010), culture includes socially inherited accomplishments of our past that serve as resources for the current life of any given social group. Culture is embedded in these social practices and communicated through language. Culture applies to both large and small groups—existing for individuals that might identify with a similar ethnicity but also for a classroom of second graders. Hence, culture emerges around a shared activity, identity, or belongingness to a group. It is a way of life, made up of day-to-day living patterns (Damen, 1987). With that said, it is important to note the following:

> Most social scientists today view culture as consisting primarily of the symbolic, ideational, and intangible aspects of human societies. The essence of a culture is not its artifacts, tools, or other tangible cultural elements but how the members of the group interpret, use,

and perceive them. It is the values, symbols, interpretations, and perspectives that distinguish one people from another in modernized societies; it is not material objects and other tangible aspects of human societies. People within a culture usually interpret the meaning of symbols, artifacts, and behaviors in the same or in similar ways (Banks, Banks, & McGee, 1989, p. 8).

Given that language serves as a tool with which culture is transmitted (Vygostky, 1962), we pay particular attention to language throughout this book, and particularly in this and the following two chapters. Cultural identity is often perceived as synonymous with the ways in which individuals use language. But for those who identify as bilingual (regardless of language proficiency), code switching—the use of two languages in a singular event—may be common. For example, in Pease-Alvarez's (2002) research, one participant noted the natural element of code switching:

> *Es usual se mezcla el español con el Ingles o el Ingles con el español. Es una costumbre…de toda California…Que está bien porque así no sabrías tan solo de un idioma, verdad? Así, si no les gusta un idioma le va el otro. Así si no entienden en uno, en alguno te entenderán. A veces yo tengo la costumbre que estoy hablando Ingles y luego…Es que me da ni sé que, que estoy hablando con un hispano…mezcleo el Ingles.* It is normal to mix Spanish with English or English with Spanish. It's a custom in all of California. It's okay because this way you don't have to know just one language, right? This way, if you don't like a language, you can go to the other one. This way, if they don't understand you, in another they will. Sometimes I have the habit that I'm going to speak English and then…It's that I don't even know that I'm speaking with a Hispanic, and I mix English (Pease-Alvarez, 2002, p. 126).

Some feel it is a product of the world students live in, one that is characterized by Spanish at home and English at school or something that youth often practice. Many parents of children who code switch view it negatively because they feel their children use it because their children are incompetent linguistically in either one or both languages (Pease-Alvarez 2002).

In the following essay, Elvis Sánchez, a Puerto Rican with a South Bronx upbringing, explores culture through the lens of language with particular attention to linguistics. He identifies and describes what he calls cultural duality and how his understanding of this was challenged through his use of language and language choice. Finally, as in chapter 4, we see how other elements of culture, such as food, carry powerful messages about cultural identity.

# English or Español? The Choice Es Mío

## by Elvis Sánchez

*There are fascinating similarities between the English and Spanish languages. As they are both European languages by origin, they share hundreds of years of history. In fact, it is those similarities that prompted me to explore their relationship. Perhaps, I thought, a little digging into their likenesses would help explain the vast cultural differences among the native speakers of both languages in the United States. Particularly, I refer to English-speaking European Americans and Spanish-speaking Latinos. The similarities between both languages can be quite evident. First, if you open side-by-side a book written in English and a book written in Spanish, you will see plainly that both languages use the Roman alphabet. Secondly, 30–40 percent of the total words in English have related words in Spanish, or cognates—words in two languages that share a similar meaning, spelling, and pronunciation ("¡colorín colorado!" 2007). Remarkably, Oller and Eilers (1982) found that a group of Spanish- and another of English-learning infants (twelve months of age) babbled alike. These similarities represent a starting point for understanding the enormous cultural differences between European Americans and Latinos possibly because in the same manner that they are bound together by their cross-cultural experiences, they are also drawn apart by each group's unique culture, a varying set of shared attitudes, values, goals, and behaviors. Perhaps that would help me comprehend why my friends and I have had negative experiences speaking both English and Spanish in different contexts. For two languages that could arguably be considered sisters or perhaps cousins at the very least, there is an ostensible tension between these two languages and their native speakers. Like two magnets of like poles, English and Spanish repel each other, my personal experiences dictate.*

*Aspiring to understand the dissimilarities through the similarities, I conducted informal research on several occasions to discover why both languages have words that are nearly identical, such as discusión and discussion or argumento and argument, and thousands of other words. One of the etymological explanations is that similarities exist because English borrowed many Latin words via French (Hock & Joseph, 1996), but there's something puzzling about that explanation. French words, when I have compared them to the Spanish words, appear truncated, such as the French word abricot (apricot), which originated from the Spanish word albaricoque, which, in turn, as do many Spanish words, originated from the Arabic* أَلْبَرْقُوق *(al barqūq). The diagram below illustrates the relationship between English and Spanish.*

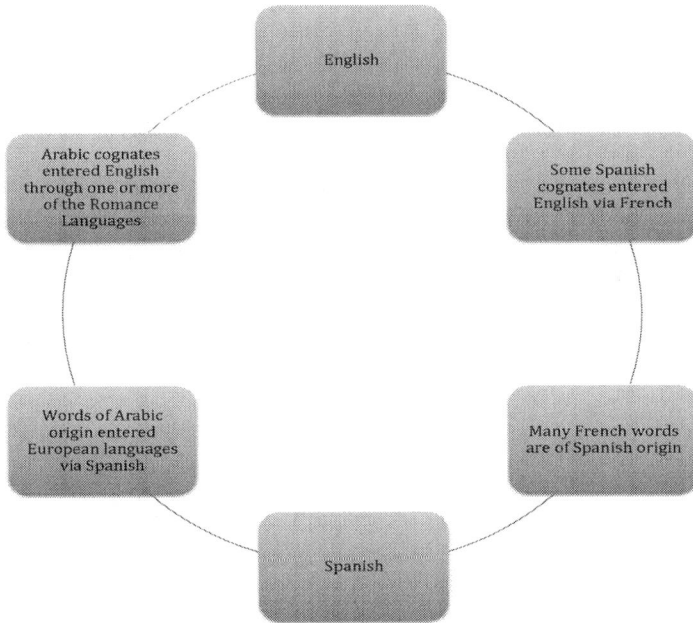

**Figure 5.1** *English/Spanish relationship*

*But that still did not explain why some English words resemble Spanish words so closely in pronunciation and spelling. Currently a graduate student at Lee University in Tennessee, I took the issue to our linguistic expert, Dr. Carolyn Dirksen. She said the following:*

97

*(1) Some words in English were borrowed from Latin, and Spanish is a descendant of Latin, so it makes sense that there would be some cognates. However, these would mainly be rather formal words or words related to the church. (2) As you say, some English words were borrowed from French, and since Spanish and French are closely related, that can explain some of the cognates. It is interesting that the Spanish and English seem more closely related than the Spanish and the French. (3) Since English and Spanish have had significant contact for several centuries, there could also be some direct borrowing of English words into Spanish and of Spanish words into English and (4) It is also possible that, through contact, the Latinate words in both languages might have changed to be more similar than either is to Latin or to French. The phonology of Spanish and English are much more similar than either is to French (personal communication, June 24, 2011).*

Dr. Dirksen points out that the speakers of English and Spanish have had close contact with each other throughout European history; they even borrowed words from each other. That type of relationship suggests a mutual respect among the English and Spanish people of Europe, and it left an imprint of their cooperation through shared words. According to Erichsen (2011), a similar sharing of words occurred in American English because many Spanish words came to us mainly from three sources. Erichsen (2011) explains:

> Many of them entered American English in the days of Mexican and/or Spanish cowboys working in what is now the US Southwest. Words of Caribbean origin entered English by way of trade. The third major source is the names of foods whose names have no English equivalent, as the intermingling of cultures has expanded our diets as well as our vocabulary.

Unfortunately, in America, despite the obvious connection between English and Spanish, the relationship between the native speakers of English (primarily Whites of diverse European ancestry) and the native speakers of Spanish (primarily Latinos originating from different countries in Latin America, particularly Mexico and the Caribbean) is often marred by cultural clashes. According to Fraga and Segura (2006), the Anglo-Protestant culture played a large role in the development of the American creed. To protect the American national identity, which is predominantly Anglocentric in nature, there is a belief *that it is "important [to have] a single national culture for the preservation of democratic institutions" (Fraga & Segura, 2006). While there is no dispute that the Anglo-Protestant culture was key in the development of the American creed, Fraga and Segura (2006) reflected that the "smaller contentions" considered in the creed proved more controversial:*

> *a national culture in the ethno-linguistic and religious sense is necessary for the formation of a successful democratic polity, that the Anglo-Protestant culture is uniquely normatively good, that the religious portion of that identity is a generally positive force in American national life, and that this culture has been historically characterized by remarkable stability, varying only modestly from its beginnings. (p. 281)*

*The American creed (as characterized above) is in direct conflict with Latino or any minority culture.*

*In the early days of US history, Howard (1993) asserted that the farther the European immigrant ancestors' cultural identities diverged from the White Anglo-Saxon Protestant image of the "real" American, the greater was the burden to assimilate. Howard (1993) contends that Jews, Catholics, Eastern Europeans, Southern Europeans, and minority religious sects received a strong message when they arrived on US soil: "Forget the home language, make sure your children don't learn to speak it, and change your name to sound more American" (Howard, 1993). However, the behavior of predominantly Roman Catholic Latino immigrants is likely perceived contrarily. Fraga and Segura (2006) claimed that there is a pervasive belief that Latinos are intentionally resisting assimilation by naturalizing (the legal process by which a foreigner is admitted to American citizenship) at extremely low rates; they maintain their native language for generations; they concentrate in particular regions and neighborhoods; and perhaps are even attempting to isolate further by building on historical claims to the Southwest to possess the land. The inaccurate beliefs held by many Americans, often resulting from generalizations and lack of information, may help explain the culture clash between English-native speakers and Spanish-native speakers from an Anglo perspective.*

**BACKGROUND KNOWLEDGE**: Latino immigrants naturalize to the United States at the lowest rates in the nation. Of the 5.4 million legal Mexican nationals in 2011, only 36 percent were naturalized, compared to 69 percent of non-Mexican immigrants. Contrary to erroneous beliefs, research shows that nine out of ten Latinos report they would become citizens if they could. In the Pew Research Center for Trends Project's 2011 National Survey of Latinos, researchers identify the barriers that hinder eligible Latinos from becoming citizens of the United States. In order to become a citizen, individuals are required to speak, read, and write English fluently, which accounts for the 26 percent who cite language and personal barriers as an obstacle. For 18 percent of Latinos, the $680 naturalization application fee and administrative barriers account for their inability to become citizens. A final factor may lie in the fact that many Mexicans may not be aware of the political change in dual citizenship. Until 1998, Mexico did not allow its citizens to hold citizenships in Mexico and the United States.

*Fraga and Segura (2006) contest the Anglo-Saxon set of beliefs, however, because the "claim assumes that the groups possess an unexpected amount of power to negotiate their place within contemporary American society, an assumption at odds with the prevailing research and common understanding" (Fraga & Segura, 2006). For example, some Latinos may be compelled to stay where they live because if they were to move to other parts of the country where Anglos are the predominant culture, they will be at a linguistic or economic disadvantage. Further, there is evidence that Latinos are indeed assimilating. Soto (2007) stated that Latinos are assimilating but in their own way, preserving much of their identity in the process. Soto (2007) offers these intriguing examples of selective assimilation: "Tamales at Christmas. Turkey and menudo at Thanksgiving. English at work and Spanish at home. Dual loyalties to the San Diego Chargers and Guadalajara Chivas. The Fourth of July. Cinco de Mayo." This phenomenon is the result of an important difference between European and Latino immigrants: Soto (2007) explained that "according to Ramos and some sociologists, Hispanics live next to their countries of origin, allowing them to maintain ties with their family, culture, and language." Howard (1993) suggested that cultural duality within a homogenous minority group is actually necessary for survival when he stated that:*

> *if you are Black, Indian, Hispanic, or Asian in the United States, daily survival depends on knowledge of white America. You need to know the*

*realities that confront you in the workplace, in dealing with government agencies, in relation to official authorities like the police. To be successful in mainstream institutions, people of color in the United States need to be bicultural, able to function in two worlds, able to play the game according to the rules established by the dominant culture.*

*Howard (1993) emphasized that the dominant group of any culture, contrariwise, has the unique luxury to choose to remain unaware of the minority cultures. "The privilege that comes with being a member of the dominant group, however, is invisible to most white Americans" (Howard, 1993). The failure of one culture to notice or acknowledge the efforts of an assimilating culture can lead to culture clash. The dynamics of modern assimilation into American society are complex and ever changing. However, resolving culture clash is not the responsibility of one group alone, according to Howard (1993): "The reality of cultural diversity in the United States is an inclusive human issue." Whites and Latinos must together be proactive to reduce our clash of cultures.*

**CRITICAL THINKING**: Think back to a time when you experienced this—you realized you were unaware of cultures outside of your own, or you were a witness to such a situation. Can you recall a time where someone was unaware or dismissive of your culture? Describe the situation. What happened? How did you feel?

*That being said, it is now time to delve into the personal experiences of my friends, my family, and me. We, too, have endured episodes of culture clash. As a second-generation bilingual Puerto Rican born and raised in New York City, English and Spanish have both been vital tools of communication since I began talking. Having family members who spoke only Spanish, my ability to speak Spanish was the only way to communicate with them. Away from home, my ability to speak English was the only way to communicate in school and other social settings. In fact my birth name, Elvis Sánchez, (an English first name and Spanish surname) attests to my bilingual lifestyle; my mother understood the value of cultural duality when she named me. Among other Puerto Ricans in my South Bronx neighborhood, there were no repercussions for choosing to speak one language or the other, and sometimes we spoke both languages simultaneously in a comical form known as Spanglish. My wife, Isabel, a second-generation bilingual Mexican born and raised in Waukegan, Illinois, (a Chicago suburb) also dabbled in some Spanglish around her Mexican and Puerto Rican friends while she was growing up. However, outside our respective ethnically homogenous spheres of familiarity, my wife and I have unfortunately experienced the ramifications of language choice.*

*It was surprising when Isabel and I learned firsthand that there are repercussions for the language we choose to speak in social settings. In fact, sometimes the ramifications manifest themselves by way of strange occurrences. More than a decade ago, my wife and I were newly married and searching for an apartment in Chattanooga, Tennessee. We sat in an office discussing an available apartment with the property manager, "Mrs. Smith," a very tall, white woman in her forties with a friendly demeanor. We talked about the apartment rules and other relevant details. A matter of concern came up that required a private conference with my wife. As we had done many times before in similar circumstances, rather than asking for a moment of privacy or walking away with my wife, we exchanged a few quick words in Spanish. The atmosphere changed immediately!*

*The friendly smile disappeared, and Mrs. Smith became enraged. She pointed her eyes at mine and began expressing herself. She said speaking Spanish in front of her was rude and disrespectful, and that she would not tolerate it under any circumstances. Naturally, I apologized (we did need the apartment). Though, I remember feeling embarrassed and a little angry. I thought, "How dare this woman dictate the language I may use!" I thought it was a matter of personal choice to use my bilingual ability as it suits me. After giving the matter some thought, nonetheless, I began to understand why the brief conversation with Isabel may have offended Mrs. Smith.*

**CRITICAL THINKING**: Why do you believe Mrs. Smith reacted the way she did? Was her reaction justified? Were Elvis and Isabel wrong to speak Spanish in front of someone who could not speak the language?

*Despite the bilingual incident with Mrs. Smith, we came to know each other and became friends. She later offered an apology for the day she prohibited my use of Spanish in her presence and even offered an explanation for her reaction. She said that intentionally omitting her from the conversation by speaking a language we assumed she did not speak is a devious tactic. We could have been saying horrible things about her for all she knew. Rather than the moment of private talk we had intended, she considered our quick switch from English to Spanish a distasteful, duplicitous action. Likewise, if I invite people to my office and they suddenly begin speaking a foreign language, bewilderment and irritation I suspect might be among my possible reactions. Subsequently, I learned an important lesson about my selective use of languages and courteousness. Excluding someone from anything is generally impolite.*

*Still, there's often an initial and underlying suspicion that being forcefully told not to speak Spanish may involve something more than a slight of manners. Indie author, Yesenia Vargas, comments on her blog (Vargas, 2014) how she was asked on separate occasions not to speak Spanish at work and at school. She recounts feeling as if a part of her identity was "inferior" and didn't "belong there." Many of my Latino friends have shared similar sentiments that when they're asked not to speak Spanish at work, school, or other venues, they feel as if they're actually being asked not to be Hispanic—in essence, speed up your assimilation. Whether the push towards cultural and linguistic assimilation is real or perceived, many Hispanics who are forbidden to use their native language react with a defensive posture aimed at protecting their cultural identity.*

**CLASSROOM CONNECTION**: There is a good possibility that you will encounter a situation in which student(s) in your classroom speak a language that you or a majority of students do not understand. In the case of recent immigrants, it might be common for another student to assist the student in their native language if other supports are not available. Given this statement about exclusion by Elvis, in what ways can you honor language and support understanding of course content while maintaining an inclusive classroom community?

*Thus, predominantly speaking English would appear to be a safer course of action. Maybe. In fact, my wife and I seldom speak Spanish at home. Our children, as a result, do not know Spanish, an issue of much contention among our Hispanic friends. "They should know Spanish," they all cry out. A couple of years ago, a friend invited us to her church, a Spanish-speaking congregation. When an elder of the church discovered that our two oldest daughters did not speak Spanish, her eyes nearly popped out of their sockets. She glared at my wife and me and hollered, "¡Eso es un pecado!" It is a sin, she said. We often clash with our Hispanic counterparts because of our controversial decision to speak only English to our kids. Truthfully, there are times I question the prudence of that decision. Isabel and I have been blessed with a new member in our family, a twenty-month-old baby girl, and to date, I refuse to talk to her in English; she will have plenty of time and opportunities to learn English. Not in the least because of social pressures and expectations, it is important to me that she learns Spanish as well.*

*Sometimes, when one is discouraged from speaking in their native tongue, it can result in a pronounced effect in the secondary language, as was the case with my friend. Spasura, a man I met several years ago in a community affair, is of Spanish descent by way of Alvernia, Putumayo, Colombia, and now lives in rural Alabama. He describes himself as a "respectable redneck." When Spasura emigrated with his family from Colombia to the United States, he was a teenager with no English-speaking ability. He once recounted how his classmates discouraged him from talking in Spanish, even threatening to harm him if he dared.*

*As a result of the bullying in school, Spasura committed himself to learning English proficiently to avoid further harassment. He developed a problem, nevertheless. He stuttered in English for several years. He did not stutter in Spanish, only in English, he reiterated. Naturally, I asked him if he knew why he stuttered in English. His best guess, he says, was that he was having trouble producing English sounds with his tongue. It is true that "the phonological system of Spanish is significantly different from that of English, particularly in the aspects of vowel sounds and sentence stress. These differences are very serious obstacles to Spanish learners being able to acquire a native-English-speaker accent" (Shoebottom, 2008). Still, I suspect there may have been more to his stuttering problem. He said he felt dumb when he stuttered because he had to repeat himself. He was very self-conscious of speaking English, and he admitted feeling anxious. It was as if everyone was waiting in anticipation to get a good laugh from his endless stuttering. Discouraged from speaking Spanish and struggling to speak English, Spasura's experience with culture clash led to a far more unique outcome. His colorful use of English, albeit somewhat convoluted, is unparalleled.*

Recently, I sent an e-mail to Spasura to let him know about my interest in writing this essay. I asked him for permission to use a sample of his writing to display his unusual use of English. He said to me, "Spasura does not find fault that you pay tribute to him today by electronically entering his modest abode in search of enlightenment and a solution to your mandrill difficulties. He too has shared in the plight of savage beasts whose wish it is to do to the faithful few unimaginable harm. Therefore, Spasura welcomes you today and invites you to grasp his appendage as we enter the mandrill constituency together in anticipation of the glory and honor we will reap in victory." That meant that he agreed, and in essence we shook hands to bind the arrangement.

His speech is no different! He talks exactly the way he writes, perpetually referring to himself in the third person. Would his use of English have been different if he had not been discouraged from talking in Spanish? Or if he had not stuttered in English? Or if he had learned English in a less stressful environment? I have to believe that his ostentatious use of language is a product of the cultural clash he experienced with his peers in his high-school days. Among the many quirks in his style of English, he refuses to spell judgment with an "e," preferring the alternate spelling of "judgement." He also admits to the intentional misuse of the indefinite article "an" and the pronoun "mine" as is evident in the preceding quote. I have the idea that Spasura may be dissenting through his use of English.

Not unlike Spasura, I have employed my own methods to protest against culture clash. For example, despite the variety of cultural cuisine in America, White and Latino cultures seem to disagree on their respective notions about the food that is considered "good" or what is considered "poor-people food." Not too long ago, I remember watching an episode of the cooking show on television, Hell's Kitchen. As the participants in the show considered which plate to create for a competitive demonstration, one chef objected to including rice in his plate because he believed that rice is a dish for poor people, not a potential award-winning dish. As an aficionado of rice, I immediately took offense. The chef's remarks about rice reminded me of another antirice sentiment some years ago. I was taking a public-speaking course in college. Our public-speaking demonstrations involved foods we enjoy. A young lady talked about her favorite food, macaroni and cheese, but not before adamantly describing her hatred for rice. I was shocked. Could it be that our cultures are as different as rice and macaroni and cheese?

*Perhaps they are. Nevertheless, on several occasions I have felt obligated to gripe about our culinary culture clash. That may be what prompted my topic of choice for a research paper in English composition a few years ago (around the same time I took the public-speaking course). The English professor asked her class to write a research paper fueled by our interests.*

*"Think about something you really like and write about it," she said.*

*Honestly, the only thing that came to mind was rice. I really like rice! Rice and beans, arroz con gandules (staple Caribbean dish: yellow rice with green pigeon peas), arroz con dulce (Puerto Rican-style rice pudding), Rice Krispies, you name it. When I met with my English professor in a required private conference to report and discuss the viability of my topic, she looked at me as if I was cracked.*

*"Elvis," she warned, "I don't think you can write your final research paper on rice."*

*I politely objected and held my ground. She looked at me incredulously. I could almost hear her thoughts. She looked at me skeptically, as if to say, "What is there to research?"*

*Surely you would like to know what happened to this rebel rice writer. I am happy to tell you through the words of a letter of recommendation from my awestricken English professor. She said in the letter:*

> *He has unusual and creative ideas for his essay topics, which he developed into papers in an organized and articulate way. For example, he wrote on "rice" for his long research paper. In the paper he explained the different kinds of rice, what makes rice disease resistant, how the protein content makes different amounts of stickiness, and how rice is cultivated. He included ideas not commonly known about rice, which is the mainstay of the diet of two-thirds of the world's population.*

*The professor's perception of rice changed after she read my research paper. She admitted in conversation she had learned a great deal about rice and appreciated her newfound understanding of the importance of rice for many cultures around the world. That was a breakthrough between our different cultures. Dissemination of knowledge is but one way to close the gap between diverse cultures. In this case, you could say that a bridge made of rice connected our two distinct cultures. For my effort, she perhaps revered rice more than she previously did, and I earned an A for my "long-grain" research paper.*

*Actually, the idea of sharing knowledge along with becoming role models and helping others understand different cultures is a significant aspect of what prompted my wife and me to pursue careers as public-school educators. We are committed teachers, as well as Hispanic role models, who have the desire to provide all students with an excellent education. Civil rights activist Cesar Chavez once said, "We need to help students and parents cherish and preserve the ethnic and cultural diversity that nourishes and strengthens this community—and this nation" (Honoring Hispanic Heritage). As public-school teachers involved with students, parents, and the community, my wife and I can help tear down the walls between Whites and Latinos, and through shared experiences we can minimize the cultural gap. In school, for example, I am concerned with creating a culturally relevant curriculum that "is crucial to academic performance and essential to culturally responsive pedagogy" (Lipton, 2012). This can be accomplished by being mindful of text selections "that include myriad voices and multiple ways of knowing, experiencing, and understanding life [so it] can help students to find and value their own voices, histories, and cultures" (Lipton, 2012).*

*In my local community, for example, I often attend with my family cultural events hosted by the predominant group, native Appalachians. It is just as important for me and my family to understand the local culture and customs as it is for us to share our own. In fact, my wife's best friend, Jenny, is a native Appalachian. Jenny and her kids often join us for dinner in eager anticipation of our delectable rice and beans—these Southerners adore Puerto Rican cuisine! A proactive stance by Latinos gives us more exposure and better opportunity to get better acquainted with our friends from other cultures.*

*Nevertheless, I wish I could say that I speak English when it suits me and Spanish when it doesn't, but the truth is English suits me the majority of the time, and it is a crucial component of my life. It drives my thoughts, it helps me thrive in academic endeavors, it helps me earn a living as an American teacher, and it helps propagate any message of import to a wider audience. Spanish, however, is equally important. It serves as a link to my cultural origins and a bridge to my Latino friends who have not yet learned English. It appeals to me to read or write something in Spanish occasionally. Both languages, if you believe they can be sisters or cousins, are conceivably interchangeable according to societal needs. We need not uphold one over the other but appreciate them for their historical bond in Europe and now in America. Being bilingual may have had its negative consequences in the past, but the ability is one that allows me to navigate across two different cultures, learn from each, and exist in each harmoniously.*

*Both languages and their native speakers are here to stay. Whether the United States ends up as a Spanish-speaking country (as some fear) or remains an English-speaking country (as is likely), it is arguably of small concern if you consider the large amount of vocabulary shared by both languages. So whether we have an argumento or argument about this issue, or a discusión or discussion, we cannot ignore the fact that Hispanics and non-Hispanics are ceaselessly connected, just as are both languages. It is ironic that my graduate advisor recently said to me in conversation, "I know English is your strength." Then later, in an unrelated conversation, he asked me to call a non-English-speaking Mexican friend to communicate a message in Spanish. Like Frank Sinatra's "Love and Marriage," when it comes to English and Spanish, it seems "you can't have one without the other." You could say the same about both Hispanic and non-Hispanic cultures. Socially and economically, our different cultures are linked to each other in American society in what should be a symbiotic relationship, not one's burden to the other.*

**About the author:** Elvis Sánchez is a second-generation Puerto Rican from the Bronx, NY. He was a Dual Language teacher in Racine, Wisconsin and currently lives in New York.

# Take It to the Classroom:

## Using Stories to Introduce Different Cultures

Classroom libraries can be a valuable resource and tool in eroding stereotypes of Latinos. Reading multicultural literature is a safe way for readers to explore the lives and experiences, cultures, or perspectives of people living in the margins.

## VARIETY OF LEVELS

Over their school career, students read at a wide variety of levels and may experience difficulty with comprehension, fluency, and/or word knowledge. Classroom libraries should have a rich foundation of at-grade-level books (i.e., fifth-grade-level reading in a fifth-grade classroom), as well as a healthy supply of texts that are a couple of reading levels below and above the target. Struggling fifth-grade readers will have options for independent reading if there are books at the third- and fourth-grade levels in the library. Some teachers organize libraries by level—designating specific areas for lower, target, and above-level reading texts. To prevent struggling readers from feeling left out or "dumb," many classroom libraries intermix books of differing levels by topic or author—and have a discreet sticker that identifies the reading level on the inside cover of each book. In addition to differing levels of texts, it would be beneficial if libraries also offer books that promote and extend students' skills in fluency, word study, and/or comprehension. Below are sample titles of books that target each area:

- Figurative-language books such as *More Parts* by Tedd Arnold, *There's a Frog in my Throat: 440 Animal Sayings a Little Bird Told Me* by Loreen Leedy, and *Amelia Bedelia* by Peggy Parish all have abundant examples of humor and figurative language.

- Tongue twisters from *The Biggest Tongue Twister Book in the World* by Gyles Brandreth are captured in this book and accented with illustrations that add to the lighthearted treatment of word study.

- Books with homophones such as *Dear Deer: A Book of Homophones* by Gene Barretta use humor to explore words that sound the same but are spelled differently.

- Books about parts of speech such as *Hairy, Scary, Ordinary: What is an Adjective?* by Brian P. Cleary use a playful text that incorporates words, pictures, and fun to give students opportunities to explore and understand different parts of speech.

- Picture books that provide opportunities to thoughtfully and authentically employ comprehension strategies, such as: *Click Clack Moo* and *Giggle Giggle Quack* by Doreen Cronin and *Too Many Tamales* by Gary Soto.

## CULTURALLY RELEVANT TEXTS

When developing a multicultural library, it is important to present a balanced representation of gender, race, religion, and social class. The Purra Belpré Award, established in 1996, is given to a high-quality piece of children's literature that represents and affirms the Latino perspective and Latino authorship. Each year, awards and honors are given to engaging and culturally relevant texts. This is a good resource for teachers who are interested in building or expanding their classroom library with quality multicultural texts. These are just a few of the many favorites that I (Tammy Oberg De La Garza) have shared with elementary, high school, and university students over the years.

### Novels

- *Dark Dude* by Oscar Hijuelos is a Cuban coming-of-age story of Rico who faces the difficulties of being a white-skinned Cubano in the 1970s. He doesn't fit in with peers in his Brooklyn High School, so he runs away and realizes life in the Midwest isn't all milk and honey.

- *Aristotle and Dante Discover the Secrets of the Universe* by Benjamin Alire Sáenz unravels a teenage Mexican's difficulties in recognizing his feelings of love for his best friend. With the help and support of family, Ari embraces his love for Dante.

- *Esperanza Rising* by Pam Muñoz Ryan is a novel set in 1930, that captures a Mexican girl's loss of wealth and her immigration to California.

- *The Revolution of Evelyn Serrano* by Sonia Manzano (Maria of *Sesame Street*) is set in New York's Puerto Rican-East Harlem barrio and follows the neighborhood activism and real-life political fight for Puerto Rican rights in 1969.

- *The Firefly Letters* by poet Margarita Engle portrays early women's rights pioneer Fredrika Bremer's perspectives of the treatment of women and slaves in 1850s Cuba.

## Picture Books

- *Martina the Beautiful Cockroach: A Cuban Folktale* by Carmen Agra Deedy is a well-loved Cuban folktale with similar versions in Puerto Rican cultures, portraying the plight of a beautiful, young cockroach on her way to choosing a kind and loving mate.

- *Chato's Kitchen* by Gary Soto and Susan Guevara follows the tales of Chato, a low-riding, cool cat from an East Los Angeles barrio and his best friend, Novio Boy.

- *My Shoes and I* by Rene Colato Lainez tells the story of a young boy and his father's arduous journey from El Salvador to the United States.

## Classroom Activities

Building a classroom multicultural library is only the first step in giving students ways to break down racial, ethnic, and cultural labels. Engaging students in learning and extension activities with the library is the main way of activating deeper thought and critical thinking about previously held stereotypes.

## Author Studies

An author study is an in-depth exploration of the life and work of one author. Author studies in the classroom are typically done on well-known and much-loved writers of children's books. Deliberately focusing a study on an author who weaves a common thread of social justice through books is a meaningful way to explore and promote themes of equality and fairness. Teachers select a prominent author of children's literature that addresses social justice/diversity/equity issues, and through read-aloud activities, book club, and independent reading activities, the class explores a good portion of the author's work. During the weeks of the author study, students will engage in the following activities:

- Make personal connections to the characters or the author
- Critically evaluate the author's characters, themes, patterns, and writing style that are threaded across the body of work
- Research and make connections between the author's life and body of work
- Trace the social-justice themes through the author's experiences and culture, finding connections and weighing the impact of the author's work in present-day society and the local community

In addition to building better reading skills, engaging students in Social Justice Author Studies builds critical thinking, improves writing skills, forges deeper understanding and attachment to books, and exposes students to a wider variety of literary voices and styles. Each of these culturally relevant materials and instructional practices further helps students understand and appreciate their own and others' experiences and cultures.

# CHAPTER 6: LANGUAGE DELIBERATIONS AND POWER

*Knowing two languages has made the world richer for me. I believe that all children should be given the opportunity of learning two or more languages when they are young, and can do so easily.*

~Alma Flor Ada~

Award winning author of books in Spanish and English for children, adults and educators, who has devoted her life to promoting social justice

The United States spreads across 3.79 million square miles of land in North America, bordered by Canada to the north and Mexico to the south. It is "home sweet home" to about 326 million people, composed of many different ethnicities and cultures (United States Census Bureau, 2017). It is a country whose native people have been displaced by large-scale immigration waves from many countries. The diversity in its people is as varied as its climate and habitats. Pause for a moment to consider this question: Beyond demographics and statistics, what is the identity of the United States? Is it the "home of the brave" or the "land of opportunity?" Is the United States a melting pot that embraces a singular American identity, or is it a patchwork quilt of unique and colorful squares—beautiful in their individual qualities as well as their contributions to the whole? The tension of US identity has lingered throughout history and still impacts families and classrooms today.

Those who believe the United States is a melting pot perceive the different origins and experiences of people to be tempered by heat, deconstructed, and mixed with other flavors to resemble the overall dish. This view does not encourage the immigrant to retain the strength or integrity of their native culture. Others see the United States as a patchwork quilt covered with unique patches of different colors, textures, and patterns. Like the national flag's white stars, blue background, and red stripes, the quilt's individual patches do not blend, nor do the shapes overlap—yet the product is a work of art.

Speakers of two languages face challenges unknown to monolinguals, as demonstrated in Chapter 5. On a daily basis, bilinguals confront social tensions and cultural assumptions about people who speak with accents. Speaking a language other than English can invite glares, comments, or confrontations from individuals who espouse the belief that America should be a melting pot with a singular language and common (blended) experience. Hearing and not understanding a bilingual speak in a foreign tongue may be offensive to a monolingual English speaker who may respond with hostility to the unknown language.

One measurable challenge faced by bilinguals is a temporary delay of language demonstration (speaking). Children are often expected to speak some basic words by eighteen months, and can say two to four word sentences by two years (CDC, 2013). Bilingual children will often speak their first words later than monolingual children (Meisel, 2004); however, the onset still falls within the normal range (Paradis, Genesee, & Crago, 2011). This can account for the sensitivity development of language discrimination between languages, meanings, and words. In addition to this temporary cost, bilinguals typically have lower formal language proficiency than monolinguals do; for example, they have smaller vocabularies and weaker access to lexical items. It is important to note though, when considering a bilingual child's total vocabulary from both languages, vocabularies of bilingual and monolingual children are the same (Hoff et al., 2012; Paradis, Genesee, & Crago 2011; Pearson et al., 1997).

Although there are hurdles, being the master of two languages has documented benefits that are personal, intellectual, and professional. An individual who can speak two languages has the ability to connect to peoples and cultures of both languages. In the case of nonnative-English speakers, maintaining fluency in the native language while learning English fosters a strong sense of identity and self-esteem through connection with family values, history, and relationships.

Research about the cognitive benefits of bilingualism demonstrates enhanced brain organization and performance. Bilingualism increases cognitive function in young adults (Costa, Hernández, & Sebatián-Gallés, 2008) and builds cognitive reserves that enable individuals to better cope with the appearance of Alzheimer's devastating symptoms (Bialystok, 2011; Bialysotk et al., 2004). The onset of dementia for bilinguals is on average four years later than monolinguals (Paradis, Genesee, & Crago, 2011). Navigating between languages increases mental flexibility from repeated right- and left-brain activation when choosing between two or more words for each concept or idea in speech and writing. Bilinguals demonstrate an increased willingness and ability to learn a third language. They show an increased analytical orientation toward language and score higher on verbal standardized tests, and math and logic skills than students who speak only one language (Kempert, Hardy, & Saalbach, 2011). Additionally, research credits bilingualism with increased memory, creativity, and problem-solving skills (Paradis. Genesee, & Crago, 2011; Schroeder & Marian, 2012). Furthermore, bilinguals show strong executive function. They are able to attend to one detail while ignoring distracting information or stimuli more effectively than their monolingual peers (Poulin-Dubois et al., 2011).

Beyond the abovementioned benefits, bilingualism offers a number of other opportunities, some of which are related to financial growth. In terms of Spanish and English, both the native-Spanish speaker and the native-English speaker can benefit from learning the opposite language and speaking it fluently. Bilingual employees are in high demand in nearly all professions and can use their skills most directly in professions such as translation or interpretation. There is increased competition for jobs in the United States, particularly for students who have recently graduated from college. This trend is most clearly illustrated by a recent study indicating that nearly half of recent college graduates are working in jobs that do not require a college degree (McKinsey & Company, 2013). This suggests that students are unable to secure the jobs most appropriate for their qualifications and are forced to take a job below their skill level. Given this trend, particularly in the United States, speaking two or more languages gives those on the job market a significant leg up, which can lead to significant financial gains. For example, in Canada those who speak both French and English have an average income nearly 10 percent higher than those who speak English only and 40 percent higher than those who speak French only (Canadian Council on Learning, 2008). Similar gains are evidenced in the United States. In particular, in Miami bilingual Hispanics earn nearly $7,000 more a year than their English-speaking peers (Fradd & Okhee, 1999).

Despite all of the advantages of being bilingual, developing fluency in two languages can both cause and alleviate conflict at home. As language is an indirect measure of culture, choosing to speak a second language may challenge the culture tied to a student's native language. According to Pease-Alvarez (2002), although parents of Spanish-speaking children often endorse the development of Spanish alongside English, the use of Spanish is often conceptualized as an important link to Mexican identity. And for many, language and identity are interchangeable. Furthermore, in Pease-Alvarez's research, "when describing what is meant for Mexican-descent parents to have children who have lost their ability or desire to speak Spanish, parents told us that such a loss would imply a loss of children's Mexican identity" (p. 120).

In some cases the extent to which Spanish is spoken at home can increase or decrease based on a number of factors. Language choice is also connected to a myriad of factors including: socialization, value placed on particular languages and forms of language use (such as code switching), language policies at school, and the formation of peer relationships (and language preferences within those relationships). For example, some Mexican-heritage parents note the difficulty of providing adequate Spanish-language support at home because of the fast-paced life in the United States and the need for one or both parents to work multiple jobs. On the contrary, when faced with schools that endorse English-Language Immersion models and discourage the use of Spanish, some families take the opportunity to require that Spanish be the only language spoken in the home. Ultimately, "Spanish-language socialization is interpreted as a means of countering threats to their children's Mexican identity" (Pease-Alvarez, 2002, p. 133), illustrating the very nature of the power of language and the underlying values language choice holds.

In the next essay, Josie Prado shares her attempts to infuse Spanish into her children's language but reveals her struggle between making a boundary-free connection with her children and building her nonnative language into their vocabulary. Josie notes that sometimes language choice comes down to which language best reflects the true self.

CRITICAL THINKING—WARM-UP STRETCH: Who are you? Reflect on your identity. Write a list of as many words and phrases that characterize and describe you. Then exchange your list with a colleague or classmate and discuss whether he or she can "see you" in your self-disclosed identity. Are your characteristics integrated, or are you a completely different person at school than you are at home?

Think of yourself in a school setting trying to understand a new language. Are there advantages to speaking more than one language? Disadvantages? Under what circumstances would fluency in two languages (or more) hinder a student? If you could speak more than one language, which would it be? Why? What is stopping you from pursuing bilingualism?

## When Home Language Obstructs Bilingualism: The Conflict of a Bilingual Mother Choosing to Raise Monolingual Children

by Josie Prado

*Language learning has been a guiding factor throughout my life in both career and personal choices. Over the years, I have had the good fortune to use my second or third language in a variety of work settings. For example, at one time, I was proficient enough in German to give guided tours at the United Nations Headquarters in New York. At a later point in my life, I learned Spanish and then interpreted for Spanish-speaking families during parent-teacher conferences while working as the English as a Second Language (ESL) Specialist in the K–12 setting. My interest in language led me to graduate school twice, once to receive a Masters of Arts in Teaching English to Speakers of Other Languages (MA—TESOL) and again, to pursue a doctoral degree in Educational Linguistics. Currently, I am writing my dissertation, which considers the impact of language choice on adolescent identity.*

*I have been told that dissertation topics emerge from a deep interest or passion the author holds for that subject, which has created an interesting juxtaposition for me. My completed dissertation will be a public endeavor, intended to add insight or information to my academic field. Yet my idea originated from private introspection and life experience. In articulating the relationship between language, culture, class, and identity, I have uncovered assumptions and questions that have been simmering in my mind for many years. The preliminary work I have done on my dissertation has enabled me to revisit life experiences with new insight to consider the seeming contradiction of my personal-language choices with my professional stance on bilingualism.*

*¿Porque no hablan tus hijos español? (Why don't your children speak Spanish?) For years, I had no answer to this question. My typical reaction was a dubious grin, a slight shrug of the shoulders, and some sort of response such as, "No se; intento pero…" (I don't know; I try but…). Indeed, it was not for lack of trying that I had not succeeded in teaching my children Spanish. For years I tried—with tapes in Spanish (stories and songs), books in Spanish—I would read to them at night. I gave mother directives in Spanish—lava la boca (wash your mouth), pon la mesa (set the table), atienda la cama (make your bed)—I tried chatting in Spanish in the car (a particular time and place for structure and consistency). I tried starting a Spanish-language literacy program on Saturdays (created for native-Spanish speakers) and brought my own children. I tried placing sticky notes all around the house with the name of the item in Spanish (espejo (mirror), libro (book), reloj (clock)).*

*After a few months, each attempt proved impossible to maintain, which generated a new wave of frustration. As an ESL Specialist and bilingual advocate, why was I arguing for bilingualism yet not promoting it in my own home? How would my children be able to identify with their Latino heritage if they were not fluent in Spanish? These questions would take me a few years of graduate school to figure out, and as I am learning, my answers continue to evolve.*

**CRITICAL THINKING**: The author perceives herself as not promoting bilingualism in her home because her children do not speak two languages; however the author does promote bilingualism through her activities and actions. What factors, do you believe, are related to the successful adaptation of two languages in childhood?

*One of the reasons my attempts failed was due to the lack of spontaneity and the need to communicate a message more complex than "set the table." With the exception of a few brief, very superficial conversations in Spanish during our car rides, my attempts to include Spanish into our daily routine involved very little meaningful communication that would get us through the day or build the parent-child bond. Ironically, this type of communication in Spanish swirled around our home. My core family of four was often accompanied by at least a few Spanish-speaking aunts, cousins, and grandparents. My children grew up hearing Spanish but rarely were spoken to in Spanish.*

**CRITICAL THINKING**: Why do you believe Josie's children were not addressed in Spanish? How do individuals make choices about language in conversational settings? What messages do these choices send?

Why would this author try to infuse the Spanish language into her children's vocabulary? Up until this point, the author has provided enough background to lead the reader to believe she believes there is a career or economic benefit to being bilingual. Would this be enough motivation for parents to employ a second language to the degree it would be required to master fluency?

*Let me explain. When I was twenty-five, I went to live in Ecuador and learned Spanish as they speak it in Quito. Marrying the eldest son of a large family, I became part of a vibrant, multigenerational Latino family and eventually, mother of two children. For five years, I lived, learned, and worked within the parameters of the Ecuadorian professional class. Until my children were born, I had spoken Spanish almost exclusively but found that gazing into my first child's face brought out nursery rhymes, songs, and motherly chatter in English. At the time, this posed no problem, since I (and those around me) assumed she would grow up bilingual, surrounded by Spanish with an English-speaking mother. After my son was born eighteen months later, I contentedly prepared myself to raise bilingual children in Quito. I had little desire to return to the United States with two toddlers; however, economic circumstances shifted for our family, and by the time my son had turned a year, we had decided to move to the United States.*

*Immigrating to my country of origin with new responsibilities and perspectives was a memorable experience. I had left the United States as a young college graduate looking for a little adventure. Five years later, I returned as a wife and mother of two young children. The transition felt chaotic and stressful. I had a Bachelor of Arts degree in German and no visible marketable skills, but as the only member of my family with permission to work, I shouldered the temporary role of primary breadwinner.*

*For the first few months, the children stayed home with their father who earnestly undertook the task of learning English. He began this task by speaking to the children only in English and attending ESL classes provided by local churches. Our new home in the United States had a small Spanish-speaking community, with only a handful of bilingual individuals holding professional positions. Most Spanish-speaking immigrants were learning English while working in restaurants, on construction sites, or as day laborers. The children's dad quickly realized the power and possibility of language. He understood that in order to extend his job opportunities to professional settings, he would have to know enough English to communicate effectively with monolingual English speakers.*

*As residency was obtained and jobs were found, our life and language patterns settled into a stable routine. The adults continued speaking Spanish to each other, but as parents we communicated with the children in English. I do not remember discussing our language patterns or making a family decision about language, so I can only explain my perspective. In those first years, I remember feeling focused on simply getting through each day. Speaking to my preschool children in Spanish required extra energy and was neither as efficient nor as effective for me, so I maintained my habit of speaking English to them.*

**CLASSROOM CONNECTION**: The author notes that language is power. In what ways might this play out in a classroom? How are children receiving messages that language is power?

*As it became apparent to others that our children were growing up as monolingual English speakers, I noticed the disapproval. Our circle of bilingual friends and family questioned and sometimes criticized my choice to speak English with my children.*

*"Oh, but you speak Spanish so well! They need to grow up bilingual!" they chided. At the time, their reproaches stung me like hornets. Because gender*

*roles within this family were clearly marked with child care falling to the mother, I realized that as the mother within this Latino family, it was expected that I raise the children to be bicultural and bilingual, regardless of whether I was the native speaker of the language or not.*

*I now understand more clearly the underlying message of their criticism. Our friends and family viewed language as the primary means to access the culture.* **In other words, in order to become bicultural, one needed to be bilingual.** *Although language helps maintain cultural and familial connections by preserving oral traditions, I would now argue that language is not the only means by which one can become bicultural. However, at the time, I felt conflicted between my actions and their cultural and linguistic expectations, but I did not yet have the knowledge to fully articulate my awareness. I knew that I resisted speaking Spanish to my children, but I did not completely understand why. (I also realized that native-Spanish speakers in the family were not speaking Spanish to the children either, but those are not my stories to tell.)*

CLASSROOM CONNECTION: With this statement in mind (*in order to become bicultural, one needed to be bilingual*), how might language be a point of division within a culture (students who are part of a culture in every other way but language, those who speak but can't write, and those who understand but can't speak)? In what ways do all of these possible compositions of biculturalism mean for students' identity in a country that primarily sees culture as singular?

*In my professional role as ESL Specialist, these criticisms made me feel hypocritical. I had studied scholarly and professional literature promoting bilingualism and fully agreed that my children, like all children, would benefit from knowing more than one language. Research (Baker, 2000, 2006; Bialystok, 2011) argues that a bilingual brain is able to think differently and more efficiently than a monolingual brain because knowing more than one language improves certain brain functions as they manage occasional conflicts between languages, making the bilingual brain "smarter" (Bhattacharjee, 2012). Additional benefits of bilingualism include cultural and familial connections; knowing more than one language creates opportunities to communicate in cross-cultural contexts and in my children's case, to converse with their Spanish-speaking grandparents.*

*When the topic of bilingualism comes up in casual conversation, it is popularly believed that young children are the most successful second-language learners and that exposure to a language is sufficient for young children to grow up bilingual. This very broad statement slides over assumptions: about what it means to be bilingual, about language varieties, about language attitudes, and about sociocultural factors and individual factors for language learners. While discussion of these topics extends far beyond the scope of this essay, I will address several ideas that have influenced my thinking professionally about the topic of home language.*

*One important distinction is whether the child's first language is the dominant language or a heritage language within his or her community. De Capua and Wintergerst (2009) define heritage language as "a language other than the dominant language that is spoken in the home, often without institutional, community, or formal support systems" (p. 6). Without support, maintaining a heritage language requires an organized and consistent effort from the family, particularly if the language is not valued in the community.*

CRITICAL THINKING: What is the dominant language that is spoken in the community where you live/work/go to school? What heritage language(s) exist within those same communities (i.e., Korean, Polish, Spanish)?
Considering the changing demographics of the United States, should schools espouse bilingualism? What would be the catalysts for change?

*Exposure to both the heritage language and the dominant language is important for young language learners. Wong Fillmore observed (1991) that young children who attended preschool or daycare and were exposed to the dominant language for many hours a day slowed their learning progress of their home language. Losing one language to replace it with another is called subtractive bilingualism (Lambert, 1977) and can have negative effects on the learner's self-esteem while causing communication difficulties at home with caregivers who speak only the heritage language.*

*Subtractive bilingualism is not the only choice; Lambert (1977) included the concept of additive bilingualism when the learner adds another language without losing the first one. Striving toward additive bilingualism, Cummins (1981) argues that developing the first language and first-language literacy skills provide a solid foundation for the child to learn his second language. As an ESL Specialist, I strongly advocated for home language and home language literacy to support ESL families' development of their children's heritage language. Believing that a strong foundation in their home language benefitted children cognitively and academically, while strengthening family connections, I lectured many well-meaning but uninformed teachers who asked ESL parents to speak a language at home they hardly knew so their children would learn the language of school a little faster.*

*Parents approach their home-language choices in many different ways. Some parents employ the "one parent, one language" strategy (De Capua & Wintergerst, 2009); other parents decide to both speak the heritage language in the home (Caldas & Caron-Caldas, 2002). Still others may choose to forgo the minority language and speak the majority language at home (Schecter & Bayley, 1997). Language choices will vary with individual families and may include factors such as language attitudes (of both the parents and the community) as well as resources such as the parent's time and energy.*

**CLASSROOM CONNECTION**: What does this mean for your students who are learning English? How can a mainstream classroom teacher support students' sense of belonging? Positive development of identity?

*In thinking about home language, I have begun to make sense of my beliefs, my actions, and their consequences. As a mother, I experienced the language of home as the language with which parents and children create their emotional bonds, relate family stories, share customs and cultural beliefs, and discover the world and how it works. These vital cultural and social interactions can be conducted in any language or combination of languages that speakers are comfortable with linguistically and as discourse. In my studies, I came to realize that the discourse of home is laden with complex issues of identity and belonging. As I disentangled academic theories of* language and identity, a straightforward reason emerged for my resistance to speaking Spanish with my children.

I can only be myself in English. The relationship I have with my children is special and precious and like no other connection I have in this world. I can only be Josie, bare and unadorned, and I am learning that I can only be this Josie in English. As much as I love languages, speaking a language other than English is like donning a cloak, a layer between me and the world. I do not want and have never wanted that layer between me and my children.

This is an important personal revelation, but it is just that—personal. This insight has helped me gain some peace about my decision to be bilingual and raise monolingual children, but how did my choices affect them? When they were in middle school, I was curious enough to do a case study with them, which began as an end-of-term assignment for a second-language literacy course. I wanted to know the connection between being bilingual and bicultural and what role their emerging proficiency in Spanish played in constructing their identities.

Within my framework for language and group belonging, Leung, Harris, and Rampton's (1997) article on language inheritance argues that ethnicity does not guarantee a certain level of proficiency in the heritage language. Indeed, they recommend replacing the term "native speaker" with the concepts of language expertise, which explains proficiency in a language; language inheritance, which refers to an individual born into the language tradition of his or her family; and language affiliation, which describes the emotional attachment the individual feels for a language and to what extent the individual associates him or herself with that language.

Using qualitative methods, I asked my children to complete literacy checklists of in-school and out-of-school activities in both Spanish and English. They created a final project answering the question, "Who am I?" and were interviewed. I also took field notes of my interactions with them. I learned that, for my children, identity and language enrich each other but do not depend on the other to exist. In other words, during their middle-school years, they felt comfortable identifying as a Latino or Latina who chooses to speak mostly English.

While this was an important revelation for me, it does not mean that they were not a little resentful for growing up monolingual. They were. My daughter understands more Spanish than my son, but she is shy about speaking. She loves *her family in Ecuador and has gone to visit several times, but her interests are leading her to places and other languages. My son, however, vociferously vented his frustrations as he struggled through Spanish III his junior year in high school. His aggravation in Spanish class exemplifies the consequences of my language choice. Neither child feels comfortably proficient in Spanish. In choosing to focus on the parent-child relationship (in English), I was also choosing to not speak Spanish with my children and not to lead them in developing their second language.*

*Perhaps for some families, this type of language choice is a nonissue. I have several friends who joyfully speak their second language with their children, but I also know many bilingual people who speak their first language with their children. As it happens, their first languages are usually heritage languages, whereas my first language was dominant in my community, creating my conflict in home-language choices.*

*I continue to believe in the benefits of bilingualism, and I am always happy (and a little envious) to hear when families raise bilingual children. I will continue to advocate for bilingualism, for the preservation of the family's or community's heritage language, and for the protection of the home language for optimal parent-child communication. All three notions are important, and it is often possible for all three to be accomplished seamlessly. Of course, some parental choices about home and heritage language will be messier than others. Having experienced the latter, I cannot offer advice, because I found the multilayered decision-making process to be intensely personal. However, I take comfort in knowing that I raised my children to appreciate a variety of cultures and the world we live in. They are capable individuals, and I trust they will pursue any language-learning opportunity (or any other learning opportunity) they wish as their futures continue to unfold.*

**About the author:** Josie Prado is an assistant professor of English Language Learner Education at the University of Alabama at Birmingham. As a teacher educator, she works throughout the state with K–12 teachers who instruct English learners in their classrooms. Her research interests include language use, identity/subjectivity, and the relationship between school and community.

# Take It to the Classroom:

## Every Teacher is a Language Instructor

In her essay, Josie Prado explores the tensions around the deliberate decision-making process she made about language selection and use for and with her children. After much reflection and professional consideration, Josie discovers that she "can only be herself in English" because it is her native language and reflects her primary heritage. It is important that we consider this idea as it applies to students in our classrooms. If students, like Josie, can only be themselves in native languages (Spanish), what happens to them when they are in academic settings conducted entirely in English?

Teachers and schools are under intense pressure to perform on standardized test measures in the dominant language (English), yet there is no consideration for supporting or measuring the academic proficiencies of Latino students' native-Spanish-language development (TESOL, 2013). Pushing Spanish speakers to learn English as quickly as possible and neglecting the native-Spanish-language development is the unspoken goal in most ESL and Bilingual classrooms. Forcing Latino students to "leave their Spanish at the door" is one method of assimilating them to English standards and academic expectations. This assimilation causes educational and relational chasms between the Latino student and Spanish-speaking family members, traditions, and values (Suárez-Orozco et al., 2011). In a sense the students are left bereft of parental or relational support and rich connections to culture. This institutionalized "orphanization" of the Latino population can be labeled as culture genocide or *subtractive schooling* (Valenzuela, 1999). This subtractive schooling is having a fatal effect on the education of Latinos in the United States. Each successive generation of Latinos in the United States achieves at academically lower levels than the previous generation (Buriel & Cardoza, 1988; Suárez-Orozco, 2001; Zsembik & Llanes, 1996).

All teachers are leaders of social justice who have a responsibility and daily opportunity to change the trajectory of this pattern (Saravia-Shore, 2008). Teachers should ask, "Will this lesson lead Latino students to associate English-only language with academic pursuits and activities, relegating Spanish to home and family settings?" Instructional practice should not force Latino students to create two identities—one that speaks English in order to be successful in school and career, and the other that speaks Spanish to fit in with family and social circles. Teachers are responsible for fostering a singular, healthy identity as well as academic development in students. It is therefore essential that instruction promote a singular persona that integrates Spanish language from home and English language in school.

## STRATEGIC INSTRUCTION

Designing classroom practice that fosters both English and native languages is attainable for ESL, bilingual, and mainstream teachers. Through strategic instruction, all teachers can make reading and texts of multiple languages and multiple cultures available to students. Teachers should model the use of research-based reading strategies with students at all levels of language competencies and provide abundant opportunities for students to utilize the strategies in a wide variety of texts—across content areas and languages. Demonstrating the strategies to students' parents or family members using texts in their native language and encouraging them to practice the strategies with children at home are powerful ways to promote home-school connections and build community.

### Prereading Strategies—Activate Background Knowledge

Understanding text is dependent on familiarity with the topic. Background knowledge of a text supports students' ability to connect new information to existing knowledge. Frequently, teachers of bilingual as well as monolingual students are challenged because student background knowledge isn't perfectly aligned with readings in textbooks. Recognizing that students have rich and unique banks of knowledge, values, and experiences different from the white middle-class background that is transmitted in school (Gee, 1996) enables teachers to value students' existing layers of background knowledge and move forward (Dyson, 2003). Using strategies to help students access the background knowledge they have and expand knowledge prior to reading can significantly support text comprehension.

A Group Frame (Brechtel, 1992) is a strategy that enables students to think about and share what they know about a topic in English and/or Spanish. Prior to reading a text selection, an overarching topic is identified, and a question is posed. If, for example the class is about to read *Abuelo y Los Tres Osos* (Abuelo and the Three Bears) (Tello & Lopez-Escriva, 1997), which is a Latino version of *Goldilocks and the Three Bears* written in both Spanish and English, the teacher might introduce the book by referencing *Goldilocks and the Three Bears*. Focusing students' attention on the subject of bears should begin with a question, "What do you know about bears?" Students are divided into groups of 3–4 to brainstorm and are asked to share their prior knowledge about bears. Groups should be arranged so that there is a variety of levels of English/Spanish proficiency within each group. After students have discussed the question, they dictate or write complete sentences on the board/overhead/SMART Board, in English or Spanish, as in the following example.

| Dictated Sentences in English Oraciones Dictados en Ingles | Dictated Sentences in Spanish Oraciones Dictados en Español |
|---|---|
| Bears are big. | Los osos son grandes. |
| Bears live in the zoo. | Los osos viven en el zoológico. |
| Bears are black. | Los osos son negros. |
| Bears are very dangerous. | Los osos son muy peligrosos. |

**Figure 6.1** *Dictated sentences in English/Spanish*

Share with students that the sentences on the board represent their background knowledge about bears and that sharing our knowledge helps us learn even more about bears. The teacher then uses the dictated sentences to scaffold student knowledge further, as in the following example.

Students read the revised sentences and discuss the changes as well as any additions to background knowledge about bears they remember as a result of the discussion. Teachers should tell students that reviewing background knowledge and information is a strategy that will help them understand texts they read in the future.

| Revised Sentences in English<br>*Oraciones Revisadas en Ingles* | Revised Sentences in Spanish<br>*Oraciones Revisadas en Español* |
|---|---|
| Bears are big and can weigh as much as 2,200 pounds. Males are bigger and heavier than females. | Los osos son grandes y pesan hasta 2.200 libras. Los machos son más grandes y más pesados que las hembras. |
| Bears live in the zoo. Wild bears live in North and South America, Europe and Asia. | Los osos viven en el zoológico. Los osos salvajes viven en Norte y Sudamérica, Europa y Asia. |
| Bears are black. They can also be brown (grizzly), white (polar) or black and white (panda). | Los osos son negros. También hay osos marrónes (pardo), blancos (polar) o blancos y negros (panda). |
| Bears can be very dangerous. Bears eat meat, but many survive on a diet of mostly vegetation. | Los osos pueden ser muy peligrosos. Los osos comen carne, pero muchos sobreviven en una dieta de vegetación en su mayoría. |

**Figure 6.2** *Revised sentences in English/Spanish*

## During Reading Strategy—Questioning

The questioning strategy called the question-answer relationship (QAR), is a powerful tool to support reading comprehension (Raphael, 1986). It can be taught quickly and then used throughout the curriculum and across grade levels in ways that enhance rather than replace planned curriculum (Oberg De La Garza, 2008). Employing this strategy is beneficial to readers of all ages but is most notably beneficial for struggling readers (Graham & Wong, 1993).

Using the QAR strategy with Latino and ESL students in mainstream, ESL, and/or bilingual settings can positively impact students' achievement and confidence in vocabulary and comprehension.

Teaching students to use the QAR strategy takes one class lesson, and then the strategy can be used by students of all reading levels, across content areas, and in any language. The first step is to introduce the four types of questions: Right There, Think and Search, Author and You, and On My Own. The Right There question is relatively simple to answer—the words used to form the question are typically in the same sentence as the answer, and we can find it one place in the text, or Right There. The Think and Search question requires a more careful approach to finding an answer. The answer to this type of question can also be found in the text; however, it is located in more than one sentence, paragraph, page, or chapter.

The answer to the third type of question, Author and You, cannot be found in the text. This question requires the reader to think about what the author has written in the text and mix it together with what the reader has experienced in his or her life. The fourth question, On My Own, is related to the content of the text; the answer cannot be found in the text. This type of question can only be answered by drawing upon previous experiences or knowledge. Figure 6.3 is a graphic organizer of the four QAR questions.

## Right There:

GO! The answer is in the text, usually easy to find. The words used to make the question and the answers are found "RIGHT THERE" in the same sentence.

## Think and Search: SLOW

DOWN! The answer is in the story, but you need to put together different parts to find it. Words for the answer come from different parts of the text (list, sequence, examples)

## Author and You: STOP! The

answer is NOT in the story. You need to think about what you already know and mix it with what you've just read. Think like the author or one of the characters.

## On My Own:

The answer is not in the story. You can even answer the question without reading the story. You need to use your own experience to answer the question.

**Figure 6.3** *QAR stoplight—types of questions*

Once students have been introduced to the four types of questions, a familiar text is then read so that students can practice the new strategy without using cognitive energy on text recall. Using the example of *Goldilocks and the Three Bears*, after students have read the text, they are organized into 4–5-member groups and asked to create one type of each of the QAR questions. Using the image below (Oberg De La Garza, 2008) can help students organize the four types of questions and serve as a reference point as they create their questions. Examples of student questions follow.

## Right There

Question: What was on the table in the kitchen?

Answer: Porridge

Explain: The answer to this question is taken directly from the story text: "On the table in the kitchen were three bowls of porridge."

## Think and Search

Question: What rooms of the cottage did Goldilocks visit?

Answer: Goldilocks visited the kitchen, the living room, and the bedroom.

Explain: There isn't one sentence in the story that answers this question. We have to think and search different parts of the story to recall which rooms Goldilocks entered.

## Author and You

Question: How did Papa Bear feel when he realized that someone had been in his home?

Answer: He was angry.

Explain: We know this because every time Papa Bear speaks, the author wrote "he growled." When animals growl, it usually means they are angry, and if somebody went into my home without permission, I would be very angry.

## On My Own

Question: Has anybody ever taken something of yours without permission?

Answer: Answers vary

Explain: We don't need to know anything about the story in order to answer this question. It's related to the story, because Goldilocks enters the bears' house, eats porridge, breaks a chair, and rests in the bears' beds without permission.

Once groups are ready to pose their questions, they are asked to critically evaluate other groups' questions to determine if the question asked was indeed the type of question identified. For example, when asked to present a Right There question, Group 1 might ask, "Whose things did Goldilocks always choose?" Another group would challenge them because the question posed is a Think and Search because it requires the reader to look at different parts of the story to connect the completely eaten porridge, broken chair, and bed with Baby Bear.

This higher level of thinking gives students the opportunity to analyze texts and think critically in either language. Practicing the skill in fiction and nonfiction texts for as little as eight weeks, students demonstrate increased text-comprehension skills (Richardson, 1994). The questioning strategy was selected to explore in depth in this text because of the opportunities it provides for peer interaction and use across various text resources and languages; however, it is only one of the major comprehension strategies students can employ. The others include visualizing, predicting, making connections, inferring, summarizing/synthesizing, and evaluating. There is an abundance of resources to learn more about each strategy, one of which is *Strategies that Work: Teaching Comprehension for Understanding and Engagement* by Harvey and Goudvis (2007).

## After Reading Strategy—Visualize and Connect

Students can extend comprehension of a text after reading in a variety of ways, but one higher-level response involves elicited personal reflection and consideration. When students draw on personal background knowledge and experiences to respond to a text, they are more successful and have increased motivation toward school (Echevarria & Graves, 2003). Typical personal-response activities in mainstream classrooms involve writing in journals, but ELL students with varying degrees of English mastery may feel inadequately prepared to use academic language in writing tasks (Altwerger & Ivener, 1994). Using alternative modalities to writing responses can extend comprehension without threatening students' sense of belonging in the classroom. One strategy that stems from visualization strategies and making connections-comprehension strategies is Sketch to Stretch (Short, Harste, & Burke, 1996). After reading a selected text that can be in any content area, genre, or language, students reflect and make connections to the text. They visualize how that connection looks if it were in a picture and then sketch the image. After students have completed their sketches, they can be invited to discuss and/or write the meaning behind their images. This type of writing is a more inviting idea for ELL students, as they have generally put much thought and energy into their drawings and are better prepared to respond with words after responding with pictures (Lenski & Ehlers-Zavala, 2004).

Providing ample opportunities for students to practice research-based reading and comprehension strategies in whatever language they feel most comfortable is beneficial for students' academic abilities and fosters a positive identity as a bilingual and bicultural individual.

# CHAPTER 7:
# LANGUAGE INSTRUCTION MODELS

*Everybody benefits from respecting, acknowledging,*
*and learning from other cultures.*

~Sonia Nieto~

Professor Emerita of Language, Literacy and Culture, University of Massachusetts,
Amherst, recognized for her scholarship, advocacy and activism

Language is a commodity we possess across the globe.
Humans use language to communicate ideas and convey emotions.
From birth, a baby's first words mark his or her presence in this world,
and the final words spoken by a loved one are cherished. Language is
a tool by which we form our identities; it is a key with which we unlock
doors. The answer to, "Do you speak English?" refers to more than a
speaker's ability to manipulate English syntax and grammar. English
mastery can represent access to community, education, career, and
power, while potentially threatening the balance of home life and
culture (as illustrated in Chapter 6). The path that native-Spanish
speakers follow to acquire the benefits of English are as varied as the
speakers themselves. Some speakers emerge triumphantly from the
English-learning journey with a fluid and powerful command of
words. Others emerge battered and forlorn, resentful of the dear price
it has cost.

## HISTORY OF BILINGUAL EDUCATION

These opposing views have created tension in US policy for decades. Because language is one of the largest indicators of culture, the tension between the melting-pot and the patchwork-quilt philosophies has spilled into the classroom. In the late 1960s, there were thirty-seven different bilingual education bills introduced in Congress. In 1968, Lyndon B. Johnson signed the Bilingual Education Act, which pronounced that children should be educated in their native tongue for a transitional year while learning English but should transfer to an English-only classroom as quickly as possible. It seemed this act would be the final word on language instruction in the classroom, but it turned out to be the beginning of a debate that endures today.

Current pressures on measurable academic performance influence curricular efforts to abandon the development of a child's native language for a faster assimilation to English. Bilingual students are able to take a standardized test sooner if they are immersed in English-only classrooms. In the short term, these students are able to grasp and demonstrate basic-level literacy skills, but long-term performance declines rapidly as literacy standards demand a deeper and more critical level of reasoning and understanding (Thomas & Collier, 2002).

## ENGLISH-LANGUAGE LEARNERS

The number of English Language Learners (ELLs) in public-school classrooms is steadily rising. From the 1997–1998 to the 2008–2009 academic year, the number of ELLs in public schools grew more than 50 percent, from 3.5 million to 5.3 million (National Clearinghouse for English Language Acquisition, 2011). More than 80 percent of these students speak Spanish (Calderon, Slavin, & Sanchez, 2011).

This rapidly expanding student population poses a unique challenge, giving educators the dual task of helping Spanish-speaking students acquire content knowledge and learn English as a second language. Furthermore, only 2.5 percent of teachers who teach ELLs in their classroom have a degree in English as a Second Language (ESL) or bilingual education (NCES, 1997). Teachers' lack of preparedness to respond to an evolving student population results, in part, in academic struggles for ELLs. The NAEP, or "Nation's Report Card," demonstrates a large achievement gap between ELL students and their peers, which is similar to the achievement gap between Latino and white students. In 2005, only 27 percent of fourth-grade ELLs' reading scores were at or above the basic reading level, compared to 75 percent of native-English speakers. By eighth grade the gap increases—29 percent of ELLs were at or above the basic reading level—a glaring contrast to the native-English speakers' achievement of 81 percent (NCES, 2010).

## LANGUAGE LEARNING THEORY

Research tells us that an ELL student can learn to communicate informally in a second language (L2) in as little as 1–2 years. It takes considerably longer for formal or academic L2 mastery—between 3–7 years (Brisk, 1998; Crawford, 1995). A student will initially rely on their native or first language (L1) to communicate with peers and teachers while acquiring vocabulary and semantics of a second language (L2). Unless their native language is instructionally fostered, the observable L1 decreases as the use of L2 emerges and becomes the academically dominant language. Students in second-language-learning programs typically transition from bilingual into mainstream classes after three years of language support. Many students spend as many as four years in a mainstream classroom before fully understanding the class discourse, vocabulary, and academic instruction. It is no wonder there is a distinct achievement gap for ELLs.

In response to the growing population of Latino students, schools are faced with the challenge of determining the most effective way to encourage language acquisition for Spanish-speaking students. Bilingual students have different levels of native-language proficiency, socioeconomic standing, and educational expectations. These factors make it very difficult for educators to determine a uniform approach that will meet the academic needs of this diverse group of students.

## ENGLISH INSTRUCTION MODELS AND TENSIONS

Since 1968, when President Lyndon Johnson acknowledged the needs of English Language Learners by signing the Bilingual Education Act, educators have debated over which method of instruction is best when educating Spanish-speaking students. Currently there are seven different models of English-language instruction: Sheltered Instruction and Structured English Immersion (SEI) programs, English as a Second Language (ESL), ESL (pull out / push in), Transitional Bilingual (Early Exit / Late Exit), and Dual Language (One Way / Two way) or Developmental Bilingual.

The debate has swirled and changed over the years, but there are essentially two camps – the subtractive model of neglecting the development of students' native language and mainly focusing on English instruction, and the additive model of expanding the academic fluency of students' native language while they learn English. What follows is an exploration of these models in relation to their subtractive or additive qualities. The Figure 7.1 below provides a visual of this continuum.

**English Language Instruction Program Model Continuum**

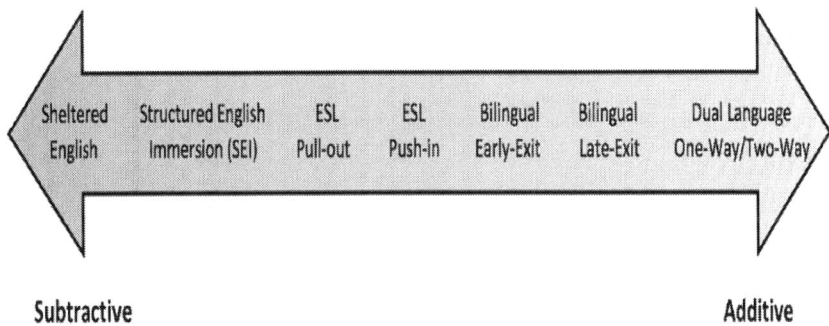

| Sheltered English | Structured English Immersion (SEI) | ESL Pull-out | ESL Push-in | Bilingual Early-Exit | Bilingual Late-Exit | Dual Language One-Way/Two-Way |

**Subtractive**                                    **Additive**

**Figure 7.1** *English Language Instruction Program Model Continuum (Oberg De La Garza & Mackinney, 2018)*

Sheltered English Instruction and Structured English Immersion (SEI) both stress a rapid increase of English exposure. Sheltered English teachers depend entirely on English, using gestures or manipulatives to foster understanding. Structured English Immersion lessons sparingly utilize students' native language only to explain or clarify English instruction (López & McEneaney, 2012).

These "sink or swim" models have historically been applied in Arizona and California, where Propositions 203 and 227[5], respectively mandated English as the only language that is used in public schools. As conceptualized in literature, SEI was designed to include native-language support for a number of years; however in practice, such support is limited and is restricted to one year (Adams & Jones, 2006).

The ESL models of English-language instruction are similar in that the goals of the programs are English proficiency and the integration of students into mainstream American culture. English is the only language used in the ESL model, which can last for 1–3 years. In ESL pull-out programs, students are pulled out of their mainstream classrooms for a specific portion of each day for ESL instruction. In ESL push-in, students remain in the mainstream classroom and receive support from an ESL teacher or an instructional aide by translating or providing clarification when needed.

The major drawback to English-only approaches is that Spanish-speaking students often feel inferior to their English-speaking peers in class due to significant differences and limitations in their reading and writing skills (Chang et al., 2007). To make matters worse, research suggests that Spanish-speaking students are not receiving the same amount of individual attention from an English-speaking teacher as their English-speaking peers receive Chang et al., 2007). Longitudinal studies on the academic achievement of Spanish-

[5] Although bilingual and dual language programs existed under Proposition 227, enough parents had to sign waivers to provide consent for their students for such programs to be provided by schools. Proposition 58, passed in 2017, effectively repeals Proposition 227 and allows students greater access to bilingual education programs.

speaking students determined that students educated in English-only programs fell into the lowest-performing academic group, rarely attained the same level of academic achievement as their English-speaking peers, and had the highest dropout and grade-retention rates (Thomas & Collier, 2002).

Unlike the previous models that use English-only, Transitional Bilingual education employs both English and Spanish during the time students participate in the program. The ultimate goals of transitional bilingual education is to "ensure students' mastery of grade-appropriate academic skills and knowledge and to facilitate and speed up the process of learning English" (Genesee, 1999, p. 19). Students are taught academic language and content in their native language in order to keep up with the students in mainstream classrooms. This approach features a self-contained setting in which students are instructed primarily in their native language for the majority of the day and in English for a small portion of the day.

The proportion of Spanish to English is determined whether the transitional bilingual program is Early Exit or Late Exit. Early Exit programs return students to mainstream English classrooms after only 1-3 years of bilingual education. Typically students exit by third grade, a benchmark year in standardized assessments (Ramirez et al., 1991). In late-exit transitional bilingual models, there is more emphasis placed on students' native language skills, requiring more time, between 5-7 years.

## DUAL LANGUAGE EDUCATION

The Dual Language (also known as Developmental Bilingual) model uses Spanish and English language in instruction for a period of 5–12 years. The goal of this model is for students to become fully bilingual, biliterate, and bicultural. Students can fit into mainstream American culture while maintaining and appreciating their native, home culture. Dual language classrooms can either be one-way or two-way. One-way classrooms consist of students from the same language or heritage language background. Two-way Immersion classrooms are populated by at least one-third non-native English speakers and at least one-third native English speakers.

Dual language education typically begins between Preschool and 1st Grade. In some dual language models, at these grade levels 80–90 percent of the instruction is in Spanish and only 10–20 percent in English. Thomas and Collier's seminal research on dual language education (2012) rationalize this emphasis on Spanish that "the rationale for [ELLs and native English speakers] initially receiving large amounts of curricular time in the minority language is that society provides a great deal of access to academic English outside of school, and much less for the minority language" (p. 14). The instructional ratio of Spanish to English gradually shifts during the primary years 80/20, 70/30, until the intermediate grades where instructional time in Spanish and English is equally split. This 50/50 balance of language instruction is maintained throughout middle and high school. Other dual language models practice a 50/50 language allocation for all grades.

Students acquire significant benefits from being enrolled in dual language programs. Spanish-speaking students in dual language programs are less likely to drop out of high school and outperform their English-speaking peers in standardized academic tests across the curriculum after 4–7 years in the dual language program (Thomas & Collier, 2002). Given that it takes 4–7 years for students to fluently master academic L2, it follows that Spanish speakers' academic and linguistic needs are most effectively addressed in educational programs that provide instruction in both languages for an extended period of time.

Dual Language is the most powerful and equitable educational model for ELLs (Lindholm-Leary & Borsato, 2006). When DL programs are sustained for at least 6 years during the elementary years, ELLs experience greater academic and linguistic success than in other English language instruction programs (Thomas & Collier, 2012). In fact, after the 6th year in DL programs, ELLs and native English speakers attain significantly higher levels of academic achievement than their counterparts in English-only classrooms. The following chart clearly outlines the achievement benefits of additive English language instruction models over subtractive approaches.

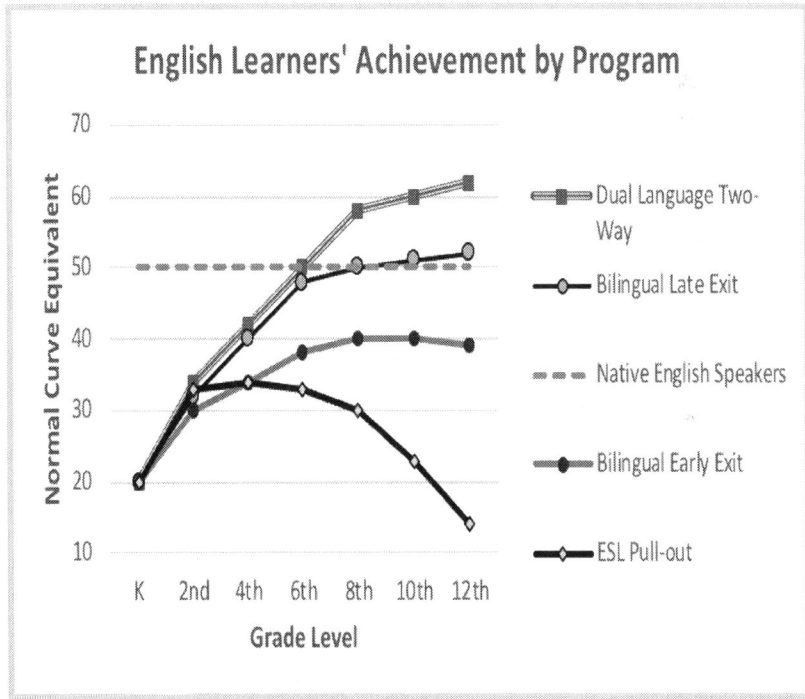

**Figure 7.2.** *ELL Achievement by Program (Thomas & Collier, 2012)*

The advantage to bilingualism and biliteracy far outweigh the lengthier period of time it takes to reach academic fluency in English. This understanding is supported by a large body of research (Bialystok & Martin, 2004; Chang et al. 2007; Duran, Roseth, & Hoffman, 2010; Goetz, 2003; Hakuta & Diaz, 1985; Kozulin, 1988). "Bilingual children have been shown to have greater metalinguistic understanding, more cognitive flexibility, better inhibitory control, and greater analogical reasoning skills than their monolingual counterparts" (Chang et al., 2007, p. 245). This work has even caught the eye of mainstream media, recently making the cover story in publications such as *TIME* magazine (Kluger, 2013). Educating Spanish-speaking children in an English-only classroom is not best practice, and programs that drop support too soon leave ELLs without sufficient academic language to ensure success as students move into more challenging content curriculum in each successive grade (Brisk, 1998).

This research is of great importance in helping policymakers realize that with sufficient time, an ELL student will achieve academic fluency in both languages, and eventually their academic performance will equal that of native-English speakers. Unfortunately the current political climate treats time as a luxury that school districts cannot afford. Present mandates require all students to take high-stakes academic tests in English, and schools are being penalized for low performance scores of language-minority students who may not be fluent in English yet. Sadly, this results in valuing standardized test achievement over authentic, life-long benefits of mastering two languages, and appreciating two cultures. Most schools operate under fear of political ramifications incited by a longer learning curve, and adhere strictly to early-exit programs that conclude within two to three years.

Table 7.1 found on the next page summarizes the different English-language instruction models by goals, timeframe, and participants (Genesee et al., 2006).

| | Sheltered Instruction/ Structured Immersion | ESL | Transitional Bilingual Early Exit | Transitional Bilingual Late Exit | Dual Language or Two-Way Immersion |
|---|---|---|---|---|---|
| **Language Goals** | Proficient in academic English | English Proficient | English Proficient | English Proficient | Bilingual, Biliterate and Bicultural |
| **Content Goals** | None | None | Minimal goals. Instruction in English | Moderate goals. Instruction in Native Language | Mastery of grade-level content in both languages |
| **Culture Goals** | Integrate into mainstream American culture | Integrate into mainstream American culture | Integrate into mainstream American culture | Integrate into mainstream American culture | Navigate and appreciate two cultures |
| **Language(s) of Instruction** | English | English | Spanish & English | Spanish & English | Spanish & English |
| **Students** | Non-Native speakers of English | Non-Native speakers of English w/ different levels of English proficiency | Non-Native speakers of English | Non-Native speakers of English | Native English Speakers & non-native English speakers |
| **Grades Served** | K-12 | K-12 | Mostly elementary | Mostly elementary | K-12 |
| **Typical Length of Participation** | 1-3 years | 1-3 years | 1-3 years | 5-7 years | 5-12 years |

**Table 7.1** *Organizational chart of English instruction models*

Regardless of which form of bilingual instruction schools choose to employ when educating native-Spanish-speaking students, it is clear that instruction in Spanish is critical. Many of the best practices in effective bilingual classrooms mirror effective practices found in mainstream classrooms. While the instructional methodologies and strategies may be similar in each of the classroom settings, the way they look and sound can be very different. Embracing the diversity of Latino students involves an open and inviting approach and calls on teacher flexibility.

This essay by Latina Reading in English teacher Laura Guzmàn-DuVernois gives the reader a playful look into her bilingual classroom where words in Spanish are as diverse as the students themselves. Laura's colorful narrative captures the value of spontaneous student discussion during planned lessons in ways that no teacher could ever anticipate. Understanding the diversity of words and meanings in a Spanish/English bilingual classroom will help mainstream classroom teachers grasp the parallel complexity of language differences facing Latino students. Observing the way that Laura responds to her students' verbal contributions to meaning making can serve as a guide for teachers who want their students to build strong, authentic, and personal vocabularies that represent their culture(s) and identity.

CRITICAL THINKING—WARM-UP STRETCH: Like physical appearance, interests, and abilities, our unique personal attributes also include language and words. From early childhood, our vocabularies carry personal meaning and connections to people, memories, and experiences. When you were a child, you might have had a unique word or name to represent something important to you, such as "MeeMaw" for Grandma or "Moony Moony" for a special moon-shaped pillow. Describe an experience when one of your special qualities was acknowledged (i.e., uncommon use of a word, special ability in school, physical quality, etc.). Who recognized these characteristics? How did you feel about your relationship with that person? How did it make you feel about yourself?

## Around Latin America in a Kite—an American Classroom

by Laura Guzmàn-DuVernois

### Circa the Urban Cohort, Orlando—some time ago...

*This story must be prefaced by explaining the duality of US classrooms in urban areas. In every classroom across the United States, the same National Anthem is proudly sung, and daily allegiance is pledged to the American flag; yet classrooms are uniquely peppered with unique, rich flavors and multicultural views. As Latino Americans, we are individuals with different backgrounds and experiences that allow us to offer diverse personalities and contribute to the essence of American life. Students in our classrooms are unique individuals in many and different sizes, shapes, and hues that make the American classroom innovative, whether in urban areas or in the middle of a beach or desert town.*

CRITICAL THINKING: Pause for a moment to consider the author's point. On the surface, it may seem common sense to acknowledge that every individual has unique qualities and experiences; however, under stressors of time, obligations, and sheer quantity of students, it may seem more efficient to categorize people and students. What different categories exist in your schema, and what assumptions are connected to each (i.e., blondes = less intelligence, uninvolved parents = uncaring parents, missing homework = unmotivated student, etc.)? How does recognizing each individual student's unique qualities, perspective, experiences, and understanding help his or her learning trajectory?

### But...First Things First

*This particular spring morning, the twenty-some students in a very diverse portable classroom were to engage in their daily adventure of mastering the art of reading and learning English. Reading may not sound exciting, funny, or remotely entertaining, but in this classroom of eight- to ten-year-olds, reading was a daily adventure of language, giggles, puzzled looks, and sometimes raised eyebrows!*

*The campus administrator was a handsome, motorcycle-riding Latino and native of Mexico. He ran the school wisely and con respeto to the student body's diversity, which derived from all parts of the world. It was not unusual to see a Russian student or to encounter newly arrived youngsters from Mexico, Cuba, Honduras, or other parts of Latin America. The student body was as diverse as the variety of Spanish dialects spoken. The campus was located in the urban middle of sunny Orlando and typical in its need of updating but rich with colorful classrooms and a caring faculty and staff.*

CRITICAL THINKING: Con respeto has strong significance in the Latino culture and community. Respect is valued highly, especially within the masculine experience, but there is another interesting connotation to the essay's reference to con respeto here. *Con Respeto: Bridging the Distances Between Culturally Diverse Families and Schools* is a 1996 ethnographic study that follows ten Mexican immigrant families' experiences in survival and learning to succeed in a new country. This study concludes that Mexican parents and families, rich with values, may be deeply undermined and injured by typical school-intervention programs, which are designed to promote school success but do not genuinely respect the values of diverse families.

**Figure 7.2** *Portable or mobile*

BACKGROUND KNOWLEDGE: Portables, mobiles, annexes, or trailers are all names for hasty expansions to school campuses. When schools become overcrowded, prefabricated school-building structures are rapidly constructed, containing temporary or permanent classrooms.

### *Portable 5, Tuesday Morning*

*If we look into one school on a given Tuesday morning, we hear the bell ring and see students scattered across campus rushing to class. Portable 5, at that time of the morning, becomes a sort of language-lab exchange, where mastering English is the common goal, regardless of background or previous experience. Wide-eyed, inquisitive faces enter the room each morning with a plethora of greetings: "buenas" and variations of "hola, Missy," depending on the day.*

*Miguel, our newest arrival from Veracruz, Mexico, seemed pensive, while Mari, a Dominican nine-year-old female student, came in with a pouty lipped expression that promised the possibility of later bilingual drama. Other students present that morning were Nena, Mari's little sister; Blanca, an inquisitive Boricua (Puerto Rican) from San Juan; Felixx, a Cuban immigrant who always looked around the classroom before rendering any type of opinion; and Nielson, always quiet as a mouse. Little Marlo, a Honduran immigrant, who had ridden La Bestia before crossing the Arizona desert to become a part of our class, and about fourteen others, became that morning's audience in what soon would become the daily novella, or soap opera, of language. In addition to our regular cast of students, our class was joined by an independent consultant to the campus. Miss White (no pun intended), a monolingual native of Indiana, was a silent observer/VIP that morning, completing the list of ingredients for the bilingual sancocho (stew) simmering in the air.*

BACKGROUND KNOWLEDGE: *La Bestia* or the Beast is the name of the cargo trains that Central Americans mount in their perilous journey to the United States. Riding atop the freight cars, hundreds or thousands of poor migrants from Mexico, Guatemala, El Salvador, Honduras, and Nicaragua have fallen to their death or have been robbed, raped, or kidnapped. Also called the "Train of Death," riding La Bestia implies a constant struggle for survival in an agonizing journey of hope, tears, and other potential dangers.

*After roll call and many well-pronounced "present" announcements, class began amid the mutter typical of a language classroom, where the day's new vocabulary word, "kite," would set off a series of unusual events in a typical elementary classroom. To an excited classroom teacher, this morning promised another adventure in learning on a beautiful sunny day.*

### A Kite in Portable 5

*Much like any other classroom, we set out to review, repeat, and talk about the new words that morning, often stopping for personal anecdotes and students' experiences as related to the lesson. "Kite," a simple noun of the English language, provided material for puzzling looks and raised hands that said, "I don't understand"...and so I explained in Spanish, how and where one used a kite, without translating the word.*

**Miguel**

*Suddenly, Miguel, shy and respectful, muttered the word papalote, which gained him some questioning glares from students of other nationalities.*

*"What?"*

*"What is that???"*

*"Papa...what?"*

153

*Patiently, Miguel explained that a papalote, in Mexico, was exactly the same thing as a kite. You flew it in the air, it was fun, and it had a long, long tail. "Yes," Miguel repeated, "a kite is a papalote, boys and girls."*

*Blanca, ever playful and informative, suddenly stood up and screamed, "Chiringa!" She explained that, "In Puerto Rico everyone flies chiringas at the beach, and it is fun, fun, fun!"*

*In back of the classroom, as if an innocent bystander, our Miss White struggled to capture the foreign words in the air and smiled as she realized that we were still talking about a kite.*

Nena          Felixx

*Nena, Mari's little sister, in her usual and stoic ways, raised her hand and said, "Chichigua. That is what a kite translates into, a plain old chichigua in the Dominican Republic."*

*Instant quiet filled the air for a few seconds. Felixx, in his predictable mysterious manner, informed the class and the guest that we were all wrong. "No, a kite was not a papalote, nor a chiringa, and definitely not a chichigua, since in Cuba everyone knew, including Fidel, that a kite translated into a barrilete," Felix concluded with satisfaction.*

CLASSROOM CONNECTION: Giving ELL students authentic opportunities to practice English is more beneficial and meaningful than preconstructed role-plays, debates, or situation conversations. Addressing the class in this more natural style can also foster skills in public speaking.

*I rushed to write all this information down on the whiteboard. Soon, Mari raised her hand, stood in front of the class, and hand on hip announced, "I am ready to share my morning adventure...and the reason why I came in pouty this morning."*

*She agreed to practice her English while sharing her adventure—but warned us that it would make more sense in Spanish. Dominican sancocho (stew), her story turned out to be.*

**Mari**

## Dominican Sancocho

*In an instant, everyone was quiet and attentive to Mari and her story. Dramatic, as her nature was, she began by telling us she woke up at 6:00 a.m. that morning and began to nag her dad about breakfast. Her papi (dad), guapo and running late for work, told her that she would get a galleta if she didn't stop the whining. In a rush, they rode to school in his guagua, and she "did not get to eat breakfast anyway, which is why I was pouty, upset, and hungry."*

*With the class almost out of time, Miguel, who was from Mexico, could not understand why Mari was upset about her papi being guapo, as he understood guapo to mean handsome, a literal translation. Mari, exasperated, told him that guapo in the Dominican Republic meant upset and that her papi was very, very guapo that morning. Scratching his head, Miguelito (little Miguel) began to unravel the mystery behind Mari's mood.*

*"OK," Miguel said, "so he was upset (guapo)...but if he offered you a galleta (cookie), why didn't you take it?"*

**Nielson**          **Miguel**          **Felixx**

"O-M-G!" Nelson let out from the back of the room. "Everyone knows that if someone offers to give you a galleta, it means they are going to hit you. Ay, Miguel, you need to learn some Spanish!"

Finally, we were all laughing in the same language of classic humor, when Miguel sheepishly raised his hand and said, "One more question…what is this about a guagua?" Felixx rolled his eyes, looked around the room, and said, "A van, Miguel. A guagua is a van!"

Miguel threw his arms up in the air and, cool and collected, informed the class, "OK…now I understand." Laughter filled the classroom as Miss White announced how impressed she was with the level of English skills the kids displayed and the priceless Spanish lesson she had just received. Shaking her head, she admitted her surprise at learning how diverse Spanish was.

CLASSROOM CONNECTIONS: As a teacher, how might you have concluded the lesson? What would be the learning objective of this activity (intended or unintended)?

### Fifteen Minutes before Lunch

As lunchtime quickly approached, portable 5 filled with noise. Students exited the classroom with quick good-byes and hasta mañanas (until tomorrow) into a beautiful Florida day. About a minute before the bell rang, Marlo raised his hand. He wanted to share one more thing about kites. "In Honduras, kites are cometas."

*Miss White was exiting the door, and when she heard this, she shook her head in disbelief and with a smile on her face, promised to come back for the next lesson. Miguelito, always last to leave the area, approached me and announced, "Today was a very good day, Missy. I learned more English, but I also learned that Spanish has many different flavors. No wonder they call your classroom sancocho (stew)! Adiòs and see you tomorrow!" On her way out, Nanda, a Chilean student, waved her good-bye and promised to bring in a kite the next day.*

CLASSROOM CONNECTIONS: Given this adventure in learning with the simple word "kite," how can a mainstream classroom benefit from varied students' experiences with language, word meanings, and memories?

### Moraleja—Is There a Moral to This Story?

*Diversity is in the fabric of our language, interaction, and definitely found within our children in classrooms across the country. For students, learning from each other is a daily adventure. For teachers, lessons can be found seated at every desk in the classroom. Most importantly, if you are reading this, embrace the richness of difference, as that is what makes you and me unique! Saludos (greetings) and next time you see a kite flying in the air, don't forget to smile, as a smile is a universal expression that needs no translation.*

**About the author:** Laura Guzmàn-DuVernois is a Latina who speaks Spanish and English with no distinguishable preference and identifies her hometown as "too many places." She earned her doctorate in Educational Leadership and Administration. She currently lives in El Paso, Texas, and is the assistant principal in an urban high school.

# Take It to the Classroom:

## Instruction that Extends Both Languages

In the essay, Laura Guzmàn-DuVernois artistically portrays a lesson with her students to demonstrate the reality that language is varied by experiences, cultural meanings, and memories. By allowing students to take center stage during the kite lesson, Laura shared a graceful example of what English learning can embody when students take on the role of active and authentic learners. When students are offering their native-language version for the word "kite," Guzmàn-DuVernois dutifully serves as a scribe to capture the variance of Spanish words that rapidly fire from every angle of the classroom. Her "backstage" role during the kite discussion clearly communicates a strong value and respect for the students' diverse experiences, voices, and perspectives.

As the lesson progressed, there was an unplanned narrative when a hungry and pouting Mari divulged the hurried interaction she had with her father that morning. In 2–3 sentences, Mari provided enough Spanish words with multiple meanings to fuel another engaging and meaningful discussion with fellow students. Through conversation and dialogue, students connected their personal understanding of words and meanings with others' definitions. Teachers who provide the time and space for the construction of meaningful scaffolds such as these provide rich opportunities for students to attach new learning to current understanding and expand their fluency and vocabulary in native (Spanish) and second languages (English).

## VOCABULARY AND FLUENCY

Laura Guzmàn-DuVernois provided a rich example of effective vocabulary and fluency instruction with the content and methodology that was portrayed in her lesson. Building fluency and vocabulary in both languages is critical for positive identity and academic development of Latino students. Research on vocabulary learning identifies levels of knowledge: fast mapping and slow or extended mapping (Swingley, 2010). Fast mapping is the process through which a new word is introduced and understood in a limited and superficial way. The student is able to read the word and recognize its meaning in a single context. Extended mapping refers to a more complex understanding of words, resulting from numerous encounters, in a number of contexts, and over a period of time. Development of the extended mapping, more beneficial level of vocabulary mastery, is the ongoing and daily responsibility of every teacher in all classrooms and content areas.

Fluency in speaking and reading is closely related to vocabulary and plays a major role in comprehension. Fluency is the ability to speak or read words without noticeable cognitive or mental effort (Laberge & Samuels, 1974). It bridges a gap between decoding and comprehension, whereby readers have mastered word recognition so automatically that it does not require conscious attention (Juel, 1991). Fluency is often measured by rate, accuracy, expression (prosody), and comprehension (Hicks, 2009; Pikulski & Chard, 2005). Providing students with resources and opportunities to practice out loud and repeated reading will expand a student's fluency capabilities. Fluency develops as a result of many opportunities to practice reading with a high degree of success. These are several types of resources students find enjoyable and effective when practicing reading for better fluency:

- Poem books such *Joyful Noise: Poems for Two Voices* by Paul Fleischman is written to be read aloud by two voices—sometimes in unison and sometimes alternating. The insect poems in this collection are irresistible and joyful.
- Reader's theater scripts by authors such as Aaron Shepard, who maintains a website with numerous high-quality Readers Theater scripts for teachers and classrooms. http://www.aaronshep.com/rt/index.html

- More—Rhyming books, folktales/fairy tale plays, and books that involve dialogue are also good resources for repeated readings and fluency practice.

Involving students in active learning and classroom participation strategically targets the development of fluency and vocabulary. This next section explores a wide variety of teaching strategies to engage all students in word study throughout each day.

Modeled Talk (Herrell, 1999)—Modeled talk is a simple and natural way of incorporating vocabulary instruction into planned lessons of any content area. During modeled talk, the teacher uses gestures, visuals, props, and demonstrations while explaining new words or ideas. This strategy gives students a visual cue or information to connect with and more accurately interpret the verbal instruction. In addition to building a feeling of belonging and community in the classroom, it gives students who are learning English the opportunity to interact with peers of more advanced levels of English fluency.

Reporting Back (Gibbons, 1993)—Giving students time and space to consider information, weigh perspectives, brainstorm, and problem solve are critical elements in the Reporting Back strategy. After a brief, whole-class introduction (up to fifteen minutes), students go off in small groups or pairs to tackle a specific task, problem, or question. While students are cooperatively engaged, teachers circulate and monitor group progress. At the end of the allotted group work time, student groups use vocabulary that is connected with the lesson to report back to the whole class their experience, findings, solutions, or reflections. It is important to note here that the students are not making a presentation to the teacher; instead, they are addressing classmates in a way that demonstrates a developing understanding and value of each other. After sufficient groups/individuals have presented, students write their reporting-back summaries reflecting new or extended thinking as a result of listening to peers' contributions. This practice helps students bridge the gap between spoken and written language, exposes them to a range of thinking, improves communication skills, cultivates confidence through prepared and voluntary presentations, and increases understanding through the verbalization of ideas (Diaz-Rico & Weed, 2002). This method of processing and communicating can be planned or spontaneous and used with students of all ages, across any subject.

Repeated Reading—Initially targeted to students with learning disabilities, researchers recognized that having students repeatedly read the same text highly impacts the reading fluency of all students (Hooks & Jones, 2002). This strategy can be used with the whole group, small group, partners, or individually with an audio recording. Depending on the level, students can reread text passages, single sentences, individual words, or even letters. Fluency drills should be done with materials that the student can read with 90–95 percent accuracy and can come from textbooks, flashcards, word walls, or student selected resources.

Vocabulary Role-Play (Jordan & Herrell, 2002)—Role-play is used to introduce and incorporate new vocabulary through dramatization. After a brief introduction of 5–10 vocabulary words and their pronunciation, spelling, surface meaning, and the ways students have seen the words used, small groups of students draft and practice mini-skits using the new words. This opportunity enables students to actively explore, internalize, make connections, and relate new words to their own lives. Students can use props and cards with the words written on them to assist in the development, writing, and/or performing of their scenarios. Watching the role-play presentations shows students how the new words may be used in different contexts, enlarging vocabulary knowledge to the extended mapping level. A technological extension of this activity would be to use iMovie, Comic Life, or Photo Booth to create videos, animated computer dictionaries, publish vocabulary books, and illustrate word porters that students can save, share, and revisit.

Multisensory Approaches—Because students must hear, see, and employ words in a variety of contexts numerous times before the words become part of the extended mapping level of understanding and ownership, teachers should provide numerous opportunities to use the words in everyday interactions.

- *Word Sort*—Organize and categorize lists of words on cards, sentence strips, and pocket charts.
- *Illustrate*—Create pictures, diagrams, displays, or videos to explain vocabulary words.
- *Word Hunt*—Find and document specific words in class lessons, conversations, television programs, magazines, and environmental print (street signs, advertisements, etc.).
- *Rhyme/Song*—Reconstruct familiar rhymes or songs (Row, row, row your boat) with word lists.
- *Games*—Make working with words enjoyable for students by playing games such as vocabulary charades, quick-draw (draw a picture representation while players guess the word), Hangman, online jeopardy template games, word searches, and more.
- *Commonyms*—is a group of three words that have a common trait. For example: car/tree/elephant = they all have trunks.
- *Visual word puzzles*—are brain teasers that translate into common phrases in English. Figure 7.3 shows examples.

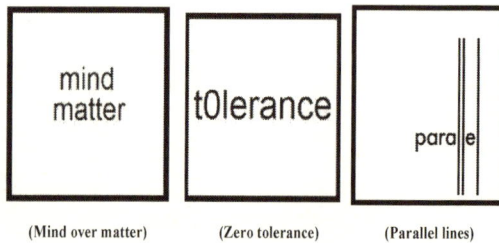

(Mind over matter)    (Zero tolerance)    (Parallel lines)

**Figure 7.3** *Visual word puzzle examples*

- *Phrase template word games*—more commonly known as Mad-Libs©, this game is a fun way for students to play with words while reinforcing types of speech. Players are prompted to offer words of specific types to fill in the blanks of a story. Teachers can use this activity with any age group and use any content-area text from books, songs, or student writing. While templates typically ask for nouns, verbs, adjectives, and adverbs, the following phrase template calls upon players to focus entirely on adjectives for their suggestions. Figure 7.4 shows an example.

---

**Adjective Template Word Game – Our Field Trip**

One day our **Bald** class went on a field trip. We went to

the **Disgusting** aquarium. We were excited to see **Sleepy**

fish and other **Haunted** creatures. Once there our **Funny**

teacher split everybody into **Gross** groups and we visited many

**Purple** exhibits. At lunchtime we were shocked to discover

**Slimy** food on the menu! After lunch, we boarded the

**Invisible** bus and enjoyed a **Smelly** trip back to school.

---

**Figure 7.4** *Phrase template word games*

- *Hink-Pink Word Riddles*—Hink-Pinks, Hinky-Pinkys, and Hinkity-Pinkitys are word riddles whose two-word answers rhyme with each other. Students or teachers can create the Hink-Pinks to challenge each other in small groups or partners. Please note that Hinky-Pinky and Hinkity-

Pinkitys are increasingly difficult to create and solve, so the creator of puzzles might offer hints, clues, or letter prompts to the answers of challenging riddles. Figure 7.5 shows several examples.

| Hink-Pink Word Riddles | |
|---|---|
| **Hink Pink**<br><br>Answer is two rhyming ONE-syllable words | **Large feline = Fat Cat**<br>**Boring choo-choo = Plain Train**<br>**50% giggle = Half Laugh** |
| **Hinky Pinky**<br><br>Answer is two rhyming TWO-syllable words | **Bathing time = Shower Hour**<br>**Admit too much = Excess Confess**<br>**Beautiful town = Pretty City** |
| **Hinkity Pinkity**<br><br>Answer is two rhyming THREE-syllable words | **2-wheeled vehicle left out for winter = Bicycle Icicle**<br>**Northern U.S. State and fruit = Montana Banana**<br>**What is the White House? = President's Residence** |

**Figure 7.5** *Hink-Pink/Hinky-Pinky word riddles*

- *Word Walls* (Tompkins, 1997)—are organized lists of words prominently displayed in the K–12 classroom for the purpose of word study and vocabulary development. One of the most prevalent lists for Word Walls includes student names and sight words. Sight words are the most frequently used words in the English language. The majority of text in English is made up of sight words, which readers need to recognize and pronounce automatically in order to achieve fluency. The Dolch Word List (Dolch, 1948) organizes 220 sight words into recommended levels and is widely used with primary grades, struggling readers, and English Language Learners. Online Dolch Word Lists websites such as http://dolchsightwords.org freely offer leveled word lists and activities that students can do individually, in groups, or with parents.

Many prekindergarten to third-grade teachers use the Dolch Word List to populate word walls in the classroom alphabetically (by first letter only). Separate word walls can be content-area specific (i.e., math word wall, science word wall), language translation (Spanish/English or English/Spanish), type of speech (i.e., fabulous adverbs, colorful adjectives, etc.), word patterns ("*ou*" words, silent "*e*" words), or simply to introduce new vocabulary words. To be effective, word walls must be dynamic, used often, grow, and change throughout the year (Allen, 1999). Here are some guidelines when using word walls:

- Classrooms can have more than one word wall. Create a permanent one with sight words and temporarily displayed lists for chapter-specific words in different subject areas, literature, or languages.

- Make words accessible by putting them where every student can see them. Large, permanent word lists can occupy a bulletin board while smaller lists can be organized on a movable poster board.

- Words should be neatly written in large, black letters on individual cards/strips, using a variety of background colors to distinguish easily confused words.

- Words should be added gradually—a general guideline is five words per week. Permanent word walls will be sparse at the beginning of the year and fill as students' vocabulary banks expand.

- Use the word lists every day to practice words, incorporating a variety of activities such as chanting, snapping, clapping, cheering, tracing, and word guessing games.

- Provide enough practice so that words are read and spelled automatically, and require that words from the wall are always spelled correctly in student writing.
- For content-area word lists, students and teachers should select words from the curriculum rather than random selections.
- Word walls should be referenced frequently so students recognize their relevance.

Giving students opportunities to contribute to word-wall lists, engage in conversations, and discuss meanings enables them to make authentic connections and shape their own understanding of new words. Whether through modeled talk, role-play, or game play, embracing the beauty and joy of words is something that teachers and students should do on a daily basis. By demonstrating an enthusiasm and curiosity for exploring new words and languages, teachers model behaviors and attitudes for students that make it safe and enjoyable for them to do the same.

# CHAPTER 8: TAKING THE DANCE FLOOR BY STORM

*With great power comes great responsibility.*

~Voltaire~

Famous French literary/philosopher writer of the 1700s Enlightenment period, whose works included *Candide*, *Oedipus*, and *Dictionnaire Philosophique*

The privilege of being a teacher carries great weight and social responsibility. You can no longer sit on the sidelines hoping you aren't asked to dance for fear of stepping on others' toes. This book has illustrated the number of ways teachers can be explicit leaders in social justice in ways that demonstrate not only a knowledge of Latino students but also of the effective teaching practices that support them. In this way, teachers not only navigate the dance between Latinos and Whites but take the lead in the dance of mixed cultures that fill classrooms and schools each year.

In this book, we guided you through six narratives portraying the multifaceted nature of Latino culture and learning. This book was deliberately designed with Culturally Sustaining Pedagogy (CSP) in mind. Culturally Sustaining Pedagogy encompasses teaching practices that are embedded in the cultural characteristics that make students different from one another and the teacher. It has the primary goal of multiculturalism and multilingualism. In two explicit ways, we embedded CSP into the book.

First, CSP served as the foundation for the pre-essay texts and pop-up prompts encouraging appropriate teacher characteristics that are the precursors to CSP. The emotional essays supported empathy and understanding of the perspectives illustrated by the essayists, challenging you to (a) reflect on beliefs about those from other cultures, (b) address your own cultural framework (and how that impacts how you view those from a similar or different cultural background), and finally, (c) build knowledge about other cultures (Rychly & Graves, 2012), particularly Latinos.

Second, in writing the book, we used Take It to the Classroom to "respond to the cultures actually present in the classroom" by "connect[ing] new information to students' background knowledge" and providing classroom exercises that "present the information in ways that respond to students' natural ways of learning" (Rychly & Graves, 2012, p. 45). As you discovered, Take It to the Classroom provided strategies for you to address relevant themes such as culture, race, ethnicity, inclusion, and language. Starting with a gentle warm-up in Chapter 2, together we explored the importance of creating an inclusive environment and turning away from damaging, culture-free approaches by directly addressing and embracing differences including race. In Chapter 3, supporting students' identity and belonging was the goal of learning experiences that were low risk/high impact. In Chapter 4, we presented guided activities to foster a culturally sustaining disposition and teaching practice. In Chapter 5, a rich collection of culturally relevant texts and books demonstrated ways to help others understand different cultures through stories. The critical need for all teachers to help bilingual English Language Learners sustain a singular identity while fostering development in both languages was accentuated in Chapter 6. Finally, Chapter 7 examined literacy-strategy instruction models for English-Language Learners, stressing the need for mainstream teachers to expand literacy skills in both languages. Exploring CSP practices has prepared you to embed instruction and materials that are sensitive to the needs of Latino students in your classroom (Rychly & Graves, 2012).

The prospect of teaching in a way that both sustains Latino students' heritage and provides opportunities for cross-cultural and cross-linguistic sharing may still seem a little frightening. Perhaps your confidence will be bolstered when you consider the massive public-school system failure in the education of Latinos. You have the proper shoes (knowledge) and have spent a considerable time warming up and practicing your dance steps. Now you hold the responsibility to step forward and ask, "May I have this dance?" Your students are waiting.

Thank you for reading *Salsa Dancing in Gym Shoes*. You can continue the discussion by scheduling a book study with the authors. For more information and other professional development opportunities, visit:

**www.SalsaDancingInGymShoes.com**

# REFERENCES

## CHAPTER 1

Achinstein, B., Ogawa, R. T., Sexton, D., & Freitas, C. (2010). Retaining teachers of color: A pressing problem and a potential strategy for "hard-to-staff" schools. *Review of Educational Research, 80*(1), 71–107.

Buchanan, B. (October, 2005). *Dropping out, dropping chances; Dropping out comes at high personal cost.* Greensboro, NC: News & Record.

Buriel, R. (1987). *Academic performance of foreign- and native-born Mexican Americans: A comparison of first-, second-, and third-generation students and parents.* Report to the Inter-University Program for Latino Research, Social Science Research Council.

Buriel, R. & Cardoza, D. (1988). Sociocultural correlates of achievement among three generations of Mexican American high school seniors. *American Educational Research Journal, 25,* 177–192.

Center for Public Education. (2013). *The United States of education: The changing demographics of the United States and their schools.* Retrieved from http://www.centerforpubliceducation.org/You-May-Also-Be-Interested-In-landing-page-level/Organizing-a-School-YMABI/The-United-States-of-education-The-changing-demographics-of-the-United-States-and-their-schools.html

Chapa, J. (1990). The myth of Hispanic progress. *Harvard Journal of Hispanic Policy Issues, 4,* 3–17.

Gándara, P. (2010). The Latino education crisis. *Educational Leadership, 67*(5), 24–30.

Gans, H. (1992). Second-generation decline: Scenarios for the economic and ethnic futures of post-1965 immigrants. *Ethnic and Racial Studies, 15*(2), 172–192.

Garza, A. V., & Crawford, L. (2005). Hegemonic multiculturalism: English immersion, ideology, and subtractive schooling. Bilingual Research Journal, *29*(3), 599–619.

Hao, L., & Woo, H.S. (2012). Distinct trajectories in the transition to adulthood: Are children of immigrants advantaged? *Child Development, 83*(5), 1623–1639.

Harper, S. R. (2012). Race without racism: How higher education researchers minimize racist institutional norms. *The Review of Higher Education, 36*(1), 9–29.

Humes, K. R., Jones, N. A., & Ramirez, R. R. (2011). *Overview of race and Hispanic origin: 2010. 2010 Census briefs.* Washington, DC: U.S. Census Bureau.

Jay, M. (2003). Critical race theory, multiculturalism, education, and the hidden curriculum of hegemony. *Multicultural Perspectives, 5*(4), 3–9.

Motel, S., & Patten, E. (2012, June 27). *The 10 largest Hispanic origin groups: Characteristics, ranking, top counties.* Retrieved from http://www.pewhispanic.org/2012/06/27/the-10-largest-hispanic-origin-groups-characteristics-rankings-top-counties/

Murillo, L. A., & Schall, J. M. (2016). "They didn't teach us well": Mexican-origin students speak out about their readiness for college literacy. *Journal of Adolescent & Adult Literacy, 60*(3), 315–323.

National Center for Educational Statistics. (2011). *Profiles of Teachers in the U.S. 2011.* U.S. Department of Education National Center for Educational Statistics. Washington DC: Institute of Education Sciences, National Center for Educational Statistics.

National Center for Educational Statistics. (2011). *Achievement Gaps: How Hispanic and White students in public schools perform in Mathematics and Reading on the National Assessment of Educational Progress.* Washington DC: Institute of Education Sciences.

National Center for Educational Statistics (2004). *English language learners in public school: 1994 and 2000.* U.S. Department of Education National Center for Educational Statistics. Washington DC: Institute of Education Sciences.

National Center for Education Statistics. (NCES). (2017). *Projections of Educational Statistics to 2025: Forty-fourth.* Washington, DC: U. S. Department of Education.

National Center for Educational Statistics. (2017). *Status and trends in the education of racial and ethnic groups- Indicator 6: Elementary and Secondary enrollment.* Retrieved from National Center for Educational Statistics on 5/29/18 https://nces.ed.gov/programs/raceindicators/indicator_rbb.asp

National Center for Educational Statistics (2018). *English language learners in public school.* U.S. Department of Education National Center for Educational Statistics. Washington DC: Institute of Education Sciences.

National Education Association (2007). *Focus on Hispanics Special Education and English Language Learners.* Washington DC: National Education Association.

Suárez-Orozco, M. (1991). Hispanic immigrant adaptation to schooling. In M. A. Biogson & J. U. Ogbu (Eds.), *Minority Status and Schooling: A Comparative Study of Immigrant and Involuntary Minorities.* New York: Garland Publishing.

Talbert-Johnson, C., & Tillman, B. (1999). Perspectives on color in teacher education programs: Prominent issues. *Journal of Teacher Education, 50*(3), 200–208.

United States Census Bureau (2016). Facts for features: Hispanic Heritage Month 2016. Release Number CB16-FF.16.

U.S. Department of Education (2016), Office of Planning, Evaluation and Policy Development, Policy and Program Studies Service, *The State of Racial Diversity in the Educator Workforce*, Washington, D.C. Accessed 6/5/18 at http://www2.ed.gov/rschstat/eval/highered/racial-diversity/state-racial-diversity- workforce.pdf

Urrieta, L. (2005). "Playing the game" versus "selling out": Chicanas and Chicanos relationship to whitestream schools. In B. K. Alexand, G. L. Anderson, & B. P. Gallegos (Eds.), *Performance theories in education: Power, pedagogy, and the politics of identity* (pp. 127–153). Mahwah, NJ: Lawrence Erlbaum and Associates.

Valenzuela, A. (1997). Mexican American youth and the politics of caring. In E. Long (Ed.). *From Sociology to Cultural Studies.* London: Blackwell.

Valenzuela, A. (1999). *Subtractive schooling: U.S.-Mexican youth and the politics of caring.* Albany, NY: State University of New York Press.

Valenzuela, A. (2003). Subtractive schooling and betrayal. *Teacher Education and Practice, 21*(4), 473–475.

Vigil, J. & Long, J. (1981). Unidirectional or nativist acculturation: Chicano paths to school achievement. *Human Organization, 40,* 273–277.

# CHAPTER 2

Cardona, P., Nicholson, B., & Fox, R. (2000). Parenting among Hispanic and Anglo-American mothers with young children. *Journal of Social Psychology, 140,* 357–365.

Cauce, A. M., & Domenech-Rodriguez, M. (2002). Latino families: Myths and realities. In J. Contreras, K. Kerns, & A Neal-Barnett (Eds.), *Latino children and families: Current research and future directions.* Westport, CT: Praeger.

Derman-Sparks, L., & Ramsey, P. G. (2006). *What if all the kids are white: Anti-bias/multicultural education for young children and families.* NY: Teachers College Press.

García Coll, C. G., Meyer, E. C., Brillon, L. (1995). Ethnic and minority parenting. In M. H. Bornstein (Ed.), *Handbook of parenting: Vol 2.: Biology and ecology of parenting* (pp. 189–209). Mahwah, NJ: Erlbaum.

Grau, J. M., Azmitia, M., & Quattlebaum, J. (2009). Latino families: Parenting, relational, and developmental processes. In F. A. Villarruel, G. Carlo, J. M. Grau, M. Azmitia, N. J. Cabrera, & T. J. Chahin (Eds.), *Handbook of Latino psychology: Development and community-based perspectives* (pp. 153–169). Thousand Oaks, CA: Sage.

Harrison, A.O., Wilson, M.N., Pine, C.J., Chan, S.Q., & Buriel, B. (1990). Family ecologies of ethnic minority children. *Child Development, 61*, 347–362.

Harwood, R. L., Schoelmerich, A., Schulze, P. A., & Gonzalez, Z. (1999). Cultural differences in maternal beliefs and behaviors: A study of middle-class Anglo and Puerto Rican mother-infant pairs in four everyday situations. *Child Development, 70*, 1005–1116.

Ispa, J., Fine, M., Halgunseth, L., Harper, S., Robinson, J., Boyce, L., et al. (2004). Maternal intrusiveness, maternal warmth, and mother-toddler relationship outcomes: Variations across low-income ethnic and acculturation groups. *Child Development, 75*, 1613–1631.

Jambunathan, S., Burts, D. C., Pierce, S. (2000). Comparisons of parenting attitudes among five ethnic groups in the United States. *Journal of Comparative Family Studies, 31*, 395–406.

Julian, T. W., McKenry, P. C., & McKelvey, M. W. (1994). Cultural variations in parenting: Perceptions of Caucasian, African American, Hispanic and Asian American parents. *Family Relations, 43*, 30–37.

Knight, G., Virdin, L., & Roosa, M. (1994). Socialization and family correlates of mental health outcomes among Hispanic and Anglo American children: Consideration of cross-ethnic scalar equivalence. *Child Development, 65*, 212–224.

Irizarry, S., & Williams, S. (2013). Lending student voice to Latino ELL migrant children's perspectives on learning. *Journal of Latinos and Education, 12*, 171–185.

Laosa, L. M. (1978). Maternal teaching strategies in Chicano families of varied educational and socioeconomic levels. *Child Development, 49*, 1129–1135.

Oberg De La Garza, T. (2013). Building strong community partnerships: Equal voice and mutual benefits. *Journal of Latinos and Education, 13(2), 120-133.*

Okagaki, L., & Frensch, P.A. (1998). Parenting and children's school achievement: A multiethnic perspective. *American Educational Research Journal, 35*, 123–144.

Padrón, Y. N., & Waxman, H. C. (1993). Teaching and learning risks associated with limited cognitive mastery in science and mathematics for limited English proficient students. In Office of Bilingual Education and Minority Languages Affairs (Eds.), *Proceedings of the third national research symposium on limited English proficient students: Focus on middle and high school issues* (Vol. 2, pp. 522–547). Washington, DC: National Clearinghouse for Bilingual Education.

Padrón, Y. N., & Waxman, H. C. (1995). Improving the teaching and learning of English language learners through instructional technology. *International Journal of Instructional Media, 23*, 341–354.

Population Resource Center. (2004, March). *Latina teen pregnancy: Problems and prevention.*

Powell, R., Cantrell, S., & Adams, S. (2001). Saving black mountain: The promise of critical literacy in a multicultural democracy. *The Reading Teacher, 54*(8).

Reese, L. S., Balzano, R., Gallimore, R., & Goldenberg, C. (1995). The concept of educación: Latino family values and American schooling. *International Journal of Educational Research, 23*, 57–81.

Ryan, C. S., Casas, J. F., Kelly-Vance, L., Ryalls, B. O., & Nero, C. (2010). Parent involvement and views of school success: The role of parents' Latino and White American culture orientations. *Psychology in the Schools, 47*(4), 319–405.

Scholmerich, A., Lamb, M., Leyendecker, B., & Fracasso, M. (1997). Mother infant teaching interaction and attachment security in Euro-American and Central-American immigrant families. *Infant Behavior and Development, 20*(2), 165–174

Sleeter, C. E. (2011). An agenda to strengthen culturally responsive pedagogy. *English Teaching: Practice and Critique, 10*(2), 7–23.

Souto-Manning, M. (2009). Educating Latino children: International perspectives and values in early education. *Childhood Education, 85*(2), 182–186.

Stern-LaRosa, C. M. (2001). Talking to your child about hatred and prejudice, Anti-Defamation League.

U.S. Census Bureau. (2001). *American's families and living arrangements.* CPR P20-537.

U.S. Census Bureau. (2010). *Households and families: 2010 census briefs.* Retrieved from http://www.census.gov/prod/cen2010/briefs/c2010br-14.pdf

Vega, W. A. (1995). The study of Latino families. In R. Zambrana (Ed.), *Understanding Latino families: Scholarship, policy, and practice* (pp. 3–17). Thousand Oaks, CA: Sage.

## CHAPTER 3

Abromitis, B.S. (1994). Bringing lives to life. Biographies in reading and the content areas. *Reading Today, 11,* 26.

Bandura, A. (1989). Human agency in Social Cognitive Theory. *American Psychologist, 44,* 1175–1184.

Banks, J. A. (2002). *An introduction to multicultural education* (3rd ed.). Boston, MA: Allyn and Bacon.

Cerda, M., Sagdeo, A., Johnson, J., & Galea, S. (2010). Genetic and environmental influences on psychiatric comorbidity: A systematic overview. *Journal of Affective Disorders, 126*(1-2), 14–38.

Deci, E. L., & Ryan, R. M. (1991). A motivational approach to self: Integration in personality. In R. Dienstbier (Ed.), *Nebraska symposium on motivation: Perspectives on motivation,* Vol. 38 (pp. 237–288). Lincoln, NE: University Of Nebraska Press.

Deci, E. L., & Ryan, R. M. (2000). The "what" and "why" of goal pursuits: Human needs and the self-determination of behavior. *Psychological Inquiry, 11*(4), 227–268.

DeFries, J. C., Plomin, R., & Fulker, D. W. (1994). *Nature and nurture during middle childhood*. Malden: Blackwell Publishing.

Furrer, C., & Skinner, E. (2003). Sense of relatedness as a factor in children's academic engagement and performance. *Journal of Educational Psychology, 95*(1), 148–162.

Goodenow, C. (1993). The psychological sense of school membership among adolescents: Scale development and educational correlates. *Psychology in the Schools, 30*, 79–90.

Lerner, R. M. (1978). Nature, nurture, and dynamic interactionism. *Human Development, 21*, 1–20.

Marsh, H. W., Barnes, J., Cairns, L., & Tidman, M. (1984). Self-description questionnaire: Age and sex effects in the structure and level of self-concept for preadolescent children. *Journal of Educational Psychology, 76*(5), 940–956.

Maslow, A. H. (1943). A theory of human motivation. *Psychological Review, 50*, 370–396.

Maslow, A. H. (1954). *Motivation and personality*. New York: Harper.

Pease-Alvarez, L. (2002). Moving beyond linear trajectories of languge shift and bilingual language socialiation. *Hispanic Journal of Behavioral Sciences 24*, 114–137.

Rosenthal, R., & Jacobson, L. (1968). *Pygmalion in the classroom*. New York: Holt, Rinehart & Winston.

Ryan, R. M., & Grolnick, W. S. (1986). Origins and pawns in the classroom: Self-report and projective assessments of individual differences in children's perceptions. *Journal of Personality and Social Psychology, 50*, 550–558.

Ryan, R. M., Stiller, J. D., & Lynch, J. H. (1994). Representations of relationships to teachers, parents, and friends as predictors of academic motivation and self-esteem. *Journal of Early Adolescence, 14*(2), 226–249.

Schein, E., & Bernstein, P. (2007). *Identical strangers: A memoir of twins separated and reunited*. New York: Random House.

# CHAPTER 4

Aronson, J., & Good, C. (2002). The development and consequences of stereotype vulnerability in adolescents. In F. Pajares & T. Urdan (Eds.), *Adolescence and education*. New York: Information Age.

Aronson, J. & Steele, C.M. (2005). Stereotypes and the fragility of human competence, motivation, and self-concept. In C. Dweck & E. Elliot (Eds.), *Handbook of Competence & Motivation*. New York, Guilford.

Baumeister, R. F., Twenge, J. W., & Nuss, C. K. (2002). Effects of social exclusion on cognitive processes: Anticipated aloneness reduces intelligent thought. *Journal of Personality and Social Psychology, 83*, 817–827.

Bhabha, H. K. (1994). *The location of culture*. NY: Routledge.

Cazden, C., & Leggett, E. (1976). Culturally responsive education: A discussion of LAU remedies, II. Prepared for the U.S. Department of Health, Education, and Welfare. National Institute of Education.

Derman-Sparks, L., Ramsey, P. G., & Edwards, J. O. (2003). *What if all the kids are white? Anti-bias multicultural education with young children and families*. New York: Teachers College Press.

Fordham, S., & Ogbu, J. (1986). Black students' school success: Coping with the "burden of acting white." *Urban Review, 18*, 176–206.

Frome, P. M., & Eccles, J. S. (1998). Parents' influence on children's achievement-related perceptions. *Journal of Personality & Social Psychology.74*, 435–452.

Gay, G. (2002). Preparing for culturally responsive teaching. *Journal of Teacher Education, 53*(2), 106–116.

Garcia, O. (2009). *Bilingual education in the 21st century: A global perspective*. Chichester, UK: Wiley-Blackwell.

Halcón, J.J. 2001. Mainstream ideology and literacy instruction for Spanish-speaking children. In *The best for our children: Critical perspectives on literacy for Latino children,* eds. M. de la Luz Reyes & J.J. Halcón, 65–77. New York: Teachers College Press.

Klingner, J.K, Artiles, A.J., Kozleski, E., Harry, B., Zion, S., Tate, W. Duran, G.Z. & Riley, D. (2005). Addressing the disproportionate representation of culturally and linguistically diverse students in special education through culturally responsive educational systems. *Education Policy Analysis Archives*, 13(38).

Ladson-Billings, G. (1995). Toward a theory of culturally relevant pedagogy. *American Educational Research Journal, 32*, 465–491.

McKown, C., & Weinstein, R. S. (2003). The development of consequences of stereotype-consciousness in middle childhood. *Child Development, 74*(2), 498–515.

Metropolitan Center for Urban Education MCUE (2008). Culturally responsive differentiated instructional strategies. New York University. Retrieved on 5/29/18 http://steinhardt.nyu.edu/scmsAdmin/uploads/005/120/Culturally%20Responsive%20Differientiated%20Instruction.pdf

Moll, L.C. (2001). The diversity of schooling: A cultural-historical approach. In M. de la Luz Reyes & J. J. Halcón (Eds.), *The best for our children: Critical perspectives on literacy for Latino children* (pp. 13–28). New York: Teachers College Press.

Morey, A., & Kilano, M. (1997). *Multicultural course transformation in higher education: A broader truth.* Needham Heights, MA: Allyn and Bacon.

Mueller, C. M., & Dweck, C. S. (1998). Praise for intelligence can undermine children's motivation and performance. *Journal of Personality and Social Psychology, 75*, 33–52.

National Center for Education Statistics (NCES). (2003). *The condition of education 2003*. Washington, DC: U. S. Department of Education.

Ogbu, J. 2001. Understanding cultural diversity and learning. In J. A. Banks & C. A. M. Banks (Eds.), *Handbook of research on multicultural education* (pp. 582–596). San Francisco: Jossey-Bass.

Paris, D. (2012). Culturally sustaining pedagogy: A needed change in stance, terminology, and practice. *Educational Researcher*, 41, 93–97.

Purdie-Vaughns, V., Steele, C., Davies, P., Ditlmann, R., & Crosby, J. (2008). Social Identity Contingencies: How diversity cues signal threat or safety for African Americans in mainstream institutions. *Journal of Personality and Social Psychology, 94*(4), 615–630.

Putnam, J. (Ed.). (1998). *Cooperative Learning and strategies for inclusion: Celebrating diversity in the classroom* (2nd ed.). Baltimore, MD: Brookes.

Richards, H., Brown, A., & Forde, T. (2006). *Addressing diversity in schools: Culturally responsive pedagogy*. Report for the National Center for Culturally Responsive Educational Systems (NCCREST); U.S. Department of Education.

Sleeter, C.E. 1995. White preservice students and multicultural education coursework. In J. M. Larking & C. E. Sleeter (Eds.), *Developing multicultural teacher education curricula* (pp. 17–29). Albany: State University of New York Press.

Solorzano, D., Ceja, M., & Yosso, T (2000). Critical race theory, racial microaggressions, and campus racial climate: The experiences of African American college students. *The Journal of Negro Education, 69*(1/2), 60–73.

Spencer, S. J., Steele, C. M., & Quinn, D. M. (1999). Stereotype threat and women's math performance. *Journal of Experimental Social Psychology, 35*, 4–28.

Steele, C. M., Spencer, S. J., & Aronson, J. (2002). Contending with group image: The psychology of stereotype and social identity threat. In M. P. Zanna (Ed.), *Advances in experimental social psychology* (Vol. 34, pp. 379–440). San Diego, CA: Academic Press.

Sue, D. W. (2010). *Microaggressions in everyday life: Race, gender, and sexual orientation*. Hoboken, NJ: Wiley

Sue, D. W., Capodilupo, C. M., & Holder, A. M. B. (2008). Racial microagressions in the life experience of Black Americans. *Professional Psychology: Research and Practice, 39*(3), 329–336.

Villegas, A. M., & Lucas, T. (2002). Preparing culturally responsive teachers: Rethinking the curriculum. *Journal of Teacher Education, 53*(13).

Wigfield, A., & Eccles, J. S. (Eds.)(2002). *Development of achievement motivation.* San Diego: Academic Press.

Wilson, T. D., & Linville, P. W. (1985). Improving the performance of college freshmen with attributional techniques. *Journal of Personality and Social Psychology, 49*(1), 287–293.

## CHAPTER 5

Agra Deedy, C. (2007). *Martina the beautiful cockroach: A Cuban folktale.* Atlanta, GA: Peachtree Publishers.

Alire Saenz, B. (2012). *Dante and Aristotle and the meaning of the universe.* New York: Simon & Schuster Books for Young Readers

Banks, J. A., & McGee, C. A., (1989). *Multicultural education.* Needham Heights, MA: Allyn & Bacon.

Colato Lainez, R. (2010). *My shoes and I.* Honesdale, PA: Boyds Mills Press.

Cole, M. (2010). What's culture got to do with it?: Educational research as a necessarily interdisciplinary enterprise. *Educational Research, 39*, 461–470.

*¡colorín colorado!.* (2007). Retrieved from http://www.colorincolorado.org/educators/background/capitalizing/

Damen, L. (1987). *Culture learning: The fifth dimension on the language classroom.* Reading, MA: Addison-Wesley.

Engle, M. (2010). *The firefly letters: A suffragette's journey to Cuba.* New York: Henry Holt & Co.

Erichsen, G. (2011). When *Spanish words become our own: adopted and borrowed words enrich English.* Retrieved on 5/29/18 from http://spanish.about.com/cs/historyofspanish/a/spanishloanword.htm

Fraga, L. R., & Segura, G. M. (2006). Culture clash? Contesting notions of American identity and the effects of Latin American immigration. *Perspective, 4*(2), 279–287.

Hijuelos, O. (2009). *Dark dude.* New York: Atheneum Books for Young Readers.

Howard, G. R. (1993). Whites in multicultural education: Rethinking our role. *Phi Delta Kappan, 75*(1), 36–41.

Hock, H. H., & Joseph, B. D. (1996). *Language history, language change, and language relationship.* New York, New York: Walter de Gruyter & Co.

Lipton, M. (2012). *Culture in the classroom.* Retrieved from http://www.tolerance.org/activity/culture-classroom

Manzano, S. (2012). *The revolution of Evelyn Serrano.* New York: Scholastic Publishing.

Munoz Ryan, P. (2002). *Esperanza rising.* New York: Scholastic Publishing.

Oller, D. K., & Eilers, R. E. (1982). Similarity of babbling in Spanish- and English-learning babies. *Journal of Child Language, 9,* 565–577.

Pease-Alvarez, L. (2002). HispanicMoving beyond linear trajectories of language shift and bilingual language socialiation. *Hispanic Journal of Behavioral Sciences, 24,* 114–137.

Pew Research Hispanic Trends Project (2011). *National Survey of Latinos.* Retrieved 11/28/2014 from http://www.pewhispanic.org/2013/09/25/2011-national-survey-of-latinos/

Pew Research Hispanic Trends Project. (2004). *Latino teens staying in high school: A challenge for all generations.* Washington, DC: Author.

Soto, H. (2007). Los latinos se asimilan bajo sus propias condiciones. *Enlace,*

Shoebottom, P. (2008). *The differences between English and Spanish.* Retrieved from http://esl.fis.edu/grammar/langdiff/spanish.htm

Soto, G., & Guevara, S. (1997). *Chato's kitchen.* London, UK: Puffin Books.

Vargas, Y. (2014). *Don't speak Spanish.* Blog retrieved on 5/29/18 from http://yeseniavargas.com

Vygotsky, L. (1962). *Thought and language.* Cambridge, MA. MIT Press.

## CHAPTER 6

Altwerger, B. & Ivener, B. (1994). Self-esteem: Access to literacy in multicultural and multilingual classrooms. In K. Spangengerg-Urbschat & R. Pritchard (Eds.), *Kids come in all languages: Reading instruction for ESL students.* Washington, DC: International Reading Association.

Baker, C. (2000). *A parents' and teachers' guide to bilingualism* (3rd ed.). Clevedon, U.K.: Multilingual Matters, Ltd.

Baker, C. (2006). *The foundations of bilingual education and bilingualism.* (4th ed.). Clevedon, U.K.: Multilingual Matters, Ltd.

Bhattacharjee, Y. (2012). "Why Bilinguals are Smarter." *The New York Times online, 5/27/12.*

Bialystok, E. (2011). Reshaping the mind: The benefits of bilingualism. *Canadian Journal of Experimental Psychology, 65*(4), 229–235.

Bialystok, E., Craik, F. I. M., Klein, R., & Viswanathan, M. (2004). Bilingualism, aging, and cognitive control: Evidence from the Simon task. *Psychology and Aging, 19,* 290–303.

Brechtel, T. (1992). *Bringing the whole together: An integrated whole-language approach for the multilingual classroom.* San Diego: Dominic.

Buriel, R., & Cardoza, D. (1988). Sociocultural correlates of achievement among three generations of Mexican American high school seniors. *American Educational Research Journal, 25*(2), 197–192.

Caldas, S., & Caron-Caldas, S. (2002). A sociolinguistic analysis of the language preferences of adolescent bilinguals: Shifting allegiances and developing identities. *Applied Linguistics, 23*(4), 490–514.

Canadian Council on Learning (2008). *Parlez-vous français? The advantages of bilingualism in Canada.*

Center for Disease Control (2013). *Developmental checklists.*

Costa, A., Hernández, M., & Sebatián-Gallés, N. (2008). Bilingualism aids conflict resolution: Evidence from the ANT task. *Cognition, 106,* 59–86.

Cummins, J. (1981). The role of primary language development in promoting educational success for language minority students. In California State Department of Education, *Schooling and language minority students: A theoretical framework* (pp. 3–50). Los Angeles, California State University, Evaluation, Dissemination and Assessment Center.

Davis Lenski, S. & Ehlers-Zavala, F. (2004). *Reading strategies for Spanish speakers.* Dubuque, IA: Kendall/Hunt Publishing.

De Capua, A., & Wintergerst, A. (2009). Second generation language maintenance and identity: A case study. *Bilingual Research Journal, 32*(1), 5–24.

Dyson, A. H. (2003). Popular literacies and the "all" children: Rethinking literacy development for contemporary childhoods. *Language Arts, 81,* 100–109.

Echevarria, J. & Graves, A. (2003). *Sheltered content instruction: Teaching English-language learners with diverse abilities* (2nd ed.). New York: Allyn and Bacon.

Fradd, S. & Okhee, L. (1999). *Creating Florida's multilingual global work force: Educational policies and practices for students learning English as a new language.* Miami, FL: Florida State University.

Gee, J. P. (1996). *Social linguistics and literacies: Ideology in discourses* (2nd ed.). London: Taylor & Francis.

Graham, L., Wong, B. (1993). Comparing two models of teaching a question answering strategy for enhancing reading comprehension: Didactic and self-instructional training. *Journal of Learning Disabilities, 26,* 270–279.

Harvey S. & Goudvis, A. (2007). *Strategies that work: Teaching comprehension for understanding and engagement.* Portland, ME: Stenhouse Publishing.

Hoff, E., Core, C., Place, S., Rumiche, R., Señor, M., & Parra, M. (2012). Dual language exposure and early bilingual development. *Journal of Child Language, 39,* 1–27.

Kempert, S., Hardy, I., & Saalbach, H. (2011). Cognitive benefits and costs of bilingualism in elementary school students: The case of mathematical word problems. *Journal of Educational Psychology, 103*(3), 547–561.

Lambert, W. E. (1977). The effects of bilingualism on the individual: Cognitive and sociocultural consequences. In P.A.Hornby (Ed.), *Bilingualism: Psychological, social and educational implications.* New York: Academic.

Lenski, S., & Ehlers-Zavala, F. (2004*). Reading Strategies for Spanish Speakers.* Dubuque, IA: Kendall/Hunt.

Leung, C., Harris, R., & Rampton, B. (1997). The idealized native speaker, reified ethnicities, and classroom realities. *TESOL Quarterly, 31*(3), 543–560.

McKinsey & Company. (2013). *Voice of the graduate.* Retrieved on 5/29/18 from https://www.mckinsey.com/industries/social-sector/our-insights/voice-of-the-graduate

Meisel, J. (2004). The Bilingual Child. In T. Bhatia & W. Ritchie (Eds.), *The Handbook of Bilingualism* (pp. 91–113). Blackwell Publishing Ltd.

Oberg De La Garza (2008). *Professional development and literacy coaching: A portrait of fostering teachers' deep understanding. Chicago, IL: University of Illinois at Chicago.*

Paradis, J., Genesee, F., & Crago, M. (2011). *Dual Language Development and Disorders: A handbook on bilingualism & second language learning.* Baltimore, MD: Paul H. Brookes Publishing.

Pearson, B.Z., Fernandez, S.C., Lewedeg, V., & Oller, D.K. (1997). The relation of input factors to lexical learning by bilingual infants. *Applied Psycholinguistics, 18,* 41–58.

Pease-Alvarez, L. (2002). Moving beyond linear trajectories on language shift and bilingual language socialization. *Hispanic Journal of Behavioral Sciences, 24,* 114–127.

Poulin-Dubois, D., Blaye, A., Coutya, J & Bialystok, E. (2011). The effects of bilingualism on toddlers' executive functioning. *Journal of Experimental Child Psychology, 108*(3), 567–579.

Raphael, T. (1986). Teaching question-answer relationships, revisited. *The Reading Teacher, 39*(6), 516–522.

Richardson, V. (1994). The consideration of teachers' beliefs. In: *Teacher change and the staff development process: A case in reading instruction.* V. Richardson (ed.), pp. 90–105. New York: Teachers College Press.

Saravia-Shore, M. (2008). Diverse teaching strategies for diverse learners. In R. Cole's (ed.) *Educating Everybody's Children: Diverse teaching strategies for diverse learners*, revised and expanded (2nd Ed.). Alexandria, VA: ASCD.

Schechter, S., & Bayley, R. (1997). Language socialization practices and cultural identity: Case studies of Mexican-descent families in California and Texas. *TESOL Quarterly, 31*(3), 513–541.

Schroeder, S., & Marian, Viorica (2012). A bilingual advantage for episodic memory in older adults. Journal of Cognitive Psychology, *24*(5), 591–601.

Short, K., Harste, J., & Burke, C. (1996). *Creating classrooms for authors and inquirers* (2nd ed.). Portsmouth, NH: Heinemann.

Suárez-Orozco, C., Birman, D., Casas, J.M., Nakamura, N., Tummala-Narra, P., & Zárate, M. (2011). *Crossroads: The psychology of immigration in the new century: Report of the 2011 APA presidential task force on immigration.* The American Psychology Association.

Suárez-Orozco, C. (2001). Psychocultural Factors in the adaptation of immigrant youth: Gendered responses. In Agosín, Marjorie (Ed.), *Women and human rights: Aglobal perspective* (pp. 170–188). Picataway, NJ: Rutgers University Press.

Tello, J. & Lopez Escriva (1997). *Abuelo Y Los Tres Osos / Abuelo and the Three Bears.* Boston, MA: Scholastic.

TESOL (2013). PreK-12 English language proficiency standards. Accessed on 5/29/18 from http://www.tesol.org/advance-the-field/standards

United States Census Bureau (2017). Population; accessed on 5/29/18, https://www.census.gov/quickfacts/fact/table/US/PST045 217

Valenzuela, A. (1999). *Subtractive schooling: U.S.-Mexican youth and the politics of caring.* Albany, NY: State University of New York Press.

Wong Fillmore, L. (1991). When learning a second language means losing the first. *Early Childhood Research Quarterly, 6,* 323–346.

Zsembik, B. A., & Llanes, D. (1996). Generational differences in educational achievement among Mexican Americans. *Social Science Quarterly, 77,* 363–375.

## CHAPTER 7

The National Clearinghouse for English Language Acquisition (2011), "The Growing Numbers of English Learner Students, 19989/99-2008/09."

Adams, M., & Jones, K. M. (2006). Unmasking the myths of structured English immersion: Why we still need bilingual educators, native language instruction, and incorporation of home culture. *Radical Teacher, 75,* 16–21.

Allen, J. (1999). *Words, words, words: Teaching vocabulary in grades 4-12.* Portland, ME: Stenhouse.

Bialystok, E., & Martin, M. M. (2004). Attention and inhibition in bilingual children: Evidence from the dimensional change card sort task. *Developmental Science, 7,* 325–339.

Brisk, M. (1998). *Bilingual education: From compensatory to quality schooling.* Mahwah, NJ: Lawrence Erlbaum Associates.

Calderon, M., Slavin, R., & Sanchez, M. (2011). Effective instruction for English learners. *The Future of Children, 21*(1), 103–127. Retrieved from http://www.jstor.org/stable/41229013

Chang, F., Crawford, D., Early, D., Bryant, D., Howes, C., Burchinal, C.,...Pianta, R. (2007). Spanish-speaking children's social and language development in pre-kindergarten classrooms. *Early Education and Development, 18*(2), 243–269.

Crawford, J. (1995). *Bilingual education: History, politics, theory and practice.* Los Angeles: Bilingual Educational Services, Inc.

Cummins, J. (1979). Cognitive/academic language proficiency, linguistic interdependence, the optimum age question and some other matters. *Working Papers on Bilingualism, 19,* 121–129.

Diaz-Rico, L., & Weed, K. (2002). *The cross-cultural, language, and academic development handbook* (2nd ed.). Boston: Allyn & Bacon.

Dolch, (1948). *Problems in reading.* Champaign, IL: Gerrard Press.

Duran, L. K., Roseth, C. J., & Hoffman, P. (2010). An experimental study comparing English-only and transitional bilingual education on Spanish-speaking preschoolers' early literacy development. *Early Childhood Research Quarterly, 25,* 207–217.

Fleischman, P. (1989). *Joyful Noise: Poems for two voices.* New York: Harper Collins.

Genesee, F. (1999). Program alternative for linguistically diverse students. *Educational Practice Report 1.* Center for Applied Linguistics: H.R. Doc. No. C2010BR-02 at 1-23 (2011).

Genesee, F., Lindholm-Leary, K., Saunders, W., & Christian, D. (2006). *Educating English language learners: A synthesis of research evidence.* New York: Cambridge University Press.

Gibbons, P. (1993). *Learning to learn in a second language.* Portsmouth, NH: Heinemann.

Goetz, P. J. (2003). The effects of bilingualism on theory of mind development. *Bilingualism: Language and Cognition, 6*(1), 1–15.

Hakuta, K., & Diaz, R. M. (1985). The relationship between degree of bilingualism and cognitive ability: A critical discussion and some new longitudinal data. In K. E. Nelson (Ed.), *Children's Language* (Vol. 5). Hillsdale, NJ: L. Erlbaum.

Herrell, A. (1999). Modeling talk to support comprehension in young children. *Kindergarten Education: Research, Theory and Practice, 3,* 29–42.

Hicks, C. P. (2009). A lesson on reading fluency learned from *The Tortoise and the Hare*. *The Reading Teacher, 63*(4), 319–323.

Hooks, P., & Jones, S. (2002). The importance of automaticity and fluency for efficient reading comprehension. *Perspectives, 28*(1).

Kluger, J. (2013, July 29). The power of the bilingual brain. *TIME Magazine, 82*(5), 1.

Jordan, M. & Herrell, A. (2002). Building comprehension bridges: A multiple strategies approach. *California Reader, 35*(4), 14–19.

Juel, C. (1991). Beginning reading. In R. Barr, M. L. Kamil, P. B. Mosenthal, & P. D. Pearson (Eds.), *Handbook of reading research* (pp. 759–788). New York: Longman.

Kozulin, A. (1988). Reality monitoring, psychological tools, and cognitive flexibility in bilinguals: Theoretical synthesis and pilot experimental investigation. *International Journal of Psychology, 23*, 79–92.

Laberge, D., & Samuels, S. (1974). Toward a theory of automatic information processing in reading. *Cognitive Psychology, 6*, 293–323.

López, F., & McEneaney, E. (2012). State implementation of language acquisition policies and reading achievement among Hispanic students. *Educational Policy, 26*, 418–464.

National Center for Education Statistics (NCES). (1997). *The condition of education 1997*. Washington, DC: U. S. Department of Education.

National Center for Education Statistics (NCES). (2010). *The condition of education 2010*. Washington, DC: U. S. Department of Education.

Oberg De La Garza, T. & Mackinney, E. (2018). Teaching English in the United States – Looking back and moving towards a brighter future. *Studies in English Language Teaching* 6(2), 86-96.

Pikulski, J. J., & Chard, D. J. (2005). Fluency: Bridge between decoding and reading comprehension. *The Reading Teacher, 58*(6), 510–519.

Ramirez, J. D., Yuen, S. D., Ramey, D. R., & Pasta, D. J. (1991). *Final report: Longitudinal study of structured English immersion strategy, early-exit, and late-exit transitional bilingual education programs for language minority children.* Retrieved from ERIC database. (ED330216)

Swingley, D. (2010). Fast mapping and slow mapping in children's word learning. *Language Learning and Development, 6,* 179–183.

Thomas, W., & Collier, V. (2002). *A national study of school effectiveness for language minority students' long-term academic achievement* [study]. From Center for Research on Education, Diversity & Excellence.

Tompkins, G. (1997). *Literacy for the 21ˢᵗ century: A balanced approach.* Upper Saddle River, NJ: Merrill/Prentice Hall.

## CHAPTER 8

Rychly, L., & Graves, E. (2012). Teacher characteristics for culturally responsive pedagogy. *Multicultural Perspectives, 14*(1), 44–49.

90273806R00120

Made in the USA
Middletown, DE
22 September 2018

# ABOUT THE AUTHORS

**Tammy Oberg De La Garza** lives in Chicago with her husband, Rey, and their college-age children, Sierra and Alex. Tammy is an associate professor and the director of the Dual Language Teacher Leadership graduate program at Roosevelt University.

**Alyson Leah Lavigne** lives in Salt Lake City with her husband, Erick, and their two sons, Leonardo and Santiago. Alyson conducts research on teacher evaluation and teaches at Utah State University in the College of Education and Human Services.

Thank you for reading *Salsa Dancing in Gym Shoes*. You can continue the discussion by scheduling a book study with the authors. For more information and other professional development opportunities, visit:

**www.SalsaDancingInGymShoes.com**